A Centenary Meditation on
a Quest for "Purification" Gone Mad

A Centenary Meditation
on
A Quest for "Purification" Gone Mad

GARDONE LECTURES (2018)

JOHN C. RAO
D. Phil., Oxford
Associate Professor of History
St. John's University

© 2019 by Arouca Press
ISBN: 978-1-9994729-7-9
© 2019 John C. Rao

All rights reserved:
No part of this book may be reproduced or transmitted,
in any form or by any means, without permission

Arouca Press
PO Box 55003
Bridgeport PO
Waterloo, ON N2J 3G0
Canada
www.aroucapress.com
Send inquiries to info@aroucapress.com

Book and cover design
by Michael Schrauzer

Cover image
"L'intérieur de Notre-Dame du Haut (Ronchamp)"
Jean-Pierre Dalbéra
(modified, from Flickr.com)

CONTENTS

PREFACE vii

1 The Peace, the War, and the Longing for Purification 1
2 Dangers on the Purification Front 9
3 Purification and Doctrine in the Interwar Era 17
4 Practical Questions and a Quest for
  Purification Gone Mad. 25
5 The Interwar Spirit on the March to the Present:
  "Catholic" Purification as the Triumph of the
  Strongest, Mindless Will 61
6 A Time Game End Game 123

BIBLIOGRAPHY. 129

PREFACE

THE TEXT THAT FOLLOWS EMBODIES THE FOUR historical conferences that I delivered to introduce the 2018 Summer Symposium of the Roman Forum—a Catholic academic organization founded by Professor Dietrich von Hildebrand to defend the Church's Magisterium against the ever-increasing assaults upon it in the wake of the Second Vatican Council. Held at Gardone Riviera on Lake Garda in northern Italy since 1993, the Summer Symposium is designed to facilitate detailed discussion of topics that have both permanent importance as well as contemporary urgency, led by a faculty coming from all continents in an atmosphere nurturing the fullness of the Catholic life: spiritual and liturgical, intellectual and fraternal, serious and joyful at one and the same time.

2018 was the centennial of the armistice concluding the "War to End All Wars", the Paris Peace Conference of the following year intended by President Woodrow Wilson of the United States to "Make the World Safe for Democracy" with the aid of a League of Nations guaranteeing peace the globe over. Unfortunately, 1918–1919 provided to be an entry into a terrible period of disruptions rather than an epoch where the lion would lie down with the lamb. The theme for the twenty-sixth annual Summer Symposium derived from these expressed hopes and real failures, with the complete picture of this strange era being painted by our international faculty under the title of "The Fittest and the Weakest: The Interwar Era, the Foundations of Late Modernity, and the Resilience of Catholic Christianity".

Gardone 2018 demonstrated that our current age—*the terminal stage of modernity*—is the child of that interwar period. Yes, it is true that contemporary modernists, like those of each previous stage in modernity's development, lay false claims to presenting something excitingly new, their Catholic brethren characteristically viewing the pontificate of Pope Francis as the latest fresh breath of the celestial zephyr. Nevertheless, all of late modernity's last gasp efforts to destroy man, nature, and culture—in order, ultimately, to make the world safe for shopping—were given their definitively elitist, willful, power-mad, and seemingly irresistible shape in the interwar years in question. This includes Catholic contributions to terminal modernism through the development of the so-called New Theology, personalism, ecumenism, and a twisted form of liturgical renewal, not to speak of the embrace of varied political ideologies of immensely destructive and dehumanizing power.

But a second and more joyful goal of the twenty-sixth Summer Symposium was that of celebrating the many powerful and endurable *achievements* of this same interwar era; achievements of unchanging value to us still today. These were accomplishments in every realm of human endeavor, from theology to literature and music; accomplishments many of which were the product of flawed but good-willed natural men striving with great talent to deal with problems of life they did not completely understand. Many Catholics participated brilliantly in such endeavors, by probing still more deeply the fullness of Sacred Tradition, and by seeking to guide those wandering in the interwar desert to the supernatural revelation and grace that could correct and perfect their already highly praiseworthy labors. All these achievements, deemed doomed to certain defeat by modernists convinced that they alone were fitted for survival, are testimonies to the innate vigor of everything Catholic and truly rational, as crucial for us to study today as for believers of the 1920s and 1930s.

As noted above, the following text only provides a schematic historical introduction to the theme in question. It is only lightly footnoted, except where direct citations require more precise documentation. Readers interested in pursuing their study of the issues in question are urged to do two things: listen to the recordings of the other speakers at the 2018 gathering, all of which are available through Keep the Faith, Inc., and consult the works provided in a brief concluding bibliography. Both, together, will provide sufficient armament for Catholic militants eager to battle for the Church in a war that, alas, cannot come to an end until the end of time.

CHAPTER I

The Peace, the War, and the Longing for Purification

Despite its claims of openness to everyone and anything, friendliness to time gone by is sorely lacking in our pluralist society, and this for very good reason indeed. Pluralism needs to destroy knowledge of the past in order to survive. Historical wisdom makes the depth and longevity of the intellectual, spiritual, and practical divisions in our daily life all too clear to those seeking to learn its lessons. Such wisdom diverts attention away from the only acceptable pluralist solution to human problems: the satisfaction of those material passions to whose endless permutations, monotonous as they ultimately really are, fallen man in his dullness seems ceaselessly attracted.

Unfortunately, we Catholics living in an all-encompassing pluralist society are ourselves subject to its soporific effects. We also have a tendency to don an historical blindfold, to focus on immediate material concerns and their time-bound explanations of current events, and, thus, to replace real intellectual judgments with shallow, pluralist-approved mantras. The result is that our own appreciation of the causes of our present ecclesiastical debacle is both too mundane as well as much too limited historically in its scope. And, sadly, this prevents us from dealing with its horrors effectively.

January 18, 2019 marked the hundredth anniversary of the beginning of the Paris Peace Conference. This conference was called to restore order after the "war to end all wars"—an "end" which endured for a mere twenty-one years, from 1918–1939. Brief though the brittle interwar period over whose birth the Paris gathering presided was, it was central to the maturation of the present-day Catholic collapse, along with the deep, pluralist-induced sleep that prevents our awakening from the living nightmare that this disintegration has engendered.

Ironically, the era gained this unhappy distinction through its nurturing of the longing of those many people who, from 1914 onwards, vocally expressed the hope that first the battlefield and then the peace to follow would somehow result in the purification of a decadent Western Civilization. Alas, all that the development of such a longing actually did achieve was to bring what was indeed a very deeply rooted Western illness guaranteeing decadence to its terminal stage. The hundredth anniversary of this quest for purification gone mad provides a valuable framework for a serious meditation upon that tragic truth.

A useful introduction to the longing for purification and its potential problems is *The Magic Mountain* of Thomas Mann, published in 1924, but set in the years leading up to the outbreak of hostilities. This novel depicts for us a prewar Europe whose spiritual illnesses and divisions ensure a paralysis represented by the frenetic but frustratingly pointless interaction of the patients of a tuberculosis sanatorium in Davos, in the Swiss Alps. I seriously doubt that Mann would have agreed with me, but as far as I am concerned, all of these inmate's woes, in one way or another, were the nefarious, long-term effect of Gnosticism, Nominalism, the Reformation, and the Enlightenment on Western Civilization. Each of these forces, from the twelfth century onwards, had contributed mightily to an attack on Reason, Faith, and legitimate authority, resulting in the "liberation" of the individual irrational will from reality. What they created, bit by bit, was the chaos of modern intellectual and physical libertinism, individual as well as social. Each has also helped to ensure that the ensuing instability would be dealt with through an appeal to one form or another of the Triumph of the Will.

Hans Castorp, the protagonist of *The Magic Mountain,* well indicates the depth of the sickness of the society in which he lives, along with the dangerous "cure" a poisonous modernity ultimately prescribes for it. He is not seriously ill at all, but chooses to join the simultaneously sybaritic and paralytic Alpine community voluntarily. Even more in need of a purpose in life than physical recovery, he and his fellow patients are only "mobilized" for action through the pressure of brute strength: to begin with, that provided by a Dutch planter from the East Indies by the name of Mynheer Peeperkorn, and, finally, by the outbreak of the First World War in 1914 itself. At the novel's end, it seems as though it is only through the self-sacrificing suffering of the totally irrational "energy" of the wretched wartime frontline experience that Castorp—and Western man as a whole—might inexplicably entertain hopes for a purification and transfiguration.

It was that same sense of awakening from a meaningless sleep to a euphoric bout of unifying, communal, vital activity, irrationally bringing purification in its train, that numerous witnesses of what the Germans called the "August Experience" testify was felt by a vocal segment of the belligerent European population in 1914. Many authors depict for us the continued impact of this theme in the frontline itself, with reference to the psychological experiences of soldiers in the trenches, as found, for example, in the early postwar writings of Ernst Jünger (1895–1998): *Storm of Steel* (1920), *The Fight as an Inner Experience* (1922), *Sturm* (1923), and *Fire and Blood* (1925).

The Roman Catholic Church might be said to have shared in this widespread hope for a purification coming from out of the war and its effects, but only in a *negative* fashion. Her wartime hope was that the insanity of the conflict might finally open the world's eyes to the accuracy of the warnings she had been giving for three quarters of a century regarding the disastrous direction taken by "modern civilization" as a whole. Those warnings were themselves rooted in a broader, nineteenth century Catholic *positive* meditation upon the full meaning of the Incarnation and the role of the Mystical Body of Christ in purifying—or, more accurately, "divinizing"—the faithful, in tandem with a social order whose authoritative aid was crucial to making men truly "sons of God".

That meditation was itself also a rediscovery; a rediscovery stimulated by the realization that Catholics had been cheated out of the fullness of their own Tradition by pastoral-minded "reformers" hiding its doctrinal treasures "under a bushel" for fear of offending the precepts of the supposedly liberating Enlightenment of the seventeenth and eighteenth centuries; an Enlightenment, once again, that had served as a conduit for the still earlier destructive influences of Gnostic, Nominalist, and Reformation character. But liberation in the Enlightenment sense was seen by nineteenth century Catholic prospectors for the *real* Tradition as producing the very opposite of what its promoters and their forbears might well have desired. On the one hand, its basic naturalism meant the imprisonment of human life in a purely earthly cell. On the other, its individualist attack on authority guaranteed that that stultifying naturalism resulted in an irrational and willful war of materialist wills against one another ending in the unjust victory of the stronger over the weaker. Catholic "traditionalists" of the 1800s argued that a triumph of the strongest irrational wills could only be reversed through a return to a Faith opening everyone and everything to purification and transformation in Christ.

The Roman Jesuit journal, *La Civiltà Cattolica*, founded in 1850, was one central contributor to the nineteenth century movement of rediscovery of the fullness of the Faith, helping mightily to shape the Syllabus of Errors of Blessed Pius IX of 1864, the subsequent development of Catholic Social Doctrine, and the entire Christian understanding of how a purification of the West might be effected along with it. To expand upon the title of one of its early articles summarizing the gist of its entire argument, either Christ will be king of the universe—with respect for Reason and with freedom for all—or man will be its king—by means of the imposition of willful, irrational force.

Achieving Christ's sovereignty in a "war of all against all" was seen by the thinkers stimulating the Catholic revival as a *militant* operation involving an "occupation" of all of the "spaces" of life: "spaces" of a spiritual, intellectual, and aesthetic, as well as political and social character. Such a practical labor, as the Council of Trent had clearly taught, had to be rooted in solid doctrine. It required a full and firm presentation of the Church's teachings to Catholics and the world at large without any apologies for the disagreements that these would arouse. Pastoral activity without strong doctrinal roots was nothing other than a "sitting duck" for manipulation of naïve believers by the innumerable representatives of the uncorrected, fallen world who form a kind of "Grand Coalition of the Status Quo", demanding an unquestioning enslavement to earthly "business as usual".

Commitment to the full message of the *Faith*, our Catholic thinkers insisted, was something quite different from adherence to the *ideologies* offered by the complex of forces slowly responsible for degrading Western Civilization. For the Catholic Faith was free from the various reductionist interpretations of existence, limited even in their grasp of the full promise of nature itself, whose unexamined acceptance earth-bound ideologies rigorously demanded. In consequence, the Faith was also open to understanding the important role that was played both by each and every aspect of earthly and supernatural life, as well as by the manifold communal authorities expressing them, and cooperating with one another in a proper hierarchy of values. It validated all of these authorities in their fruitful work for the ultimate benefit of individuals whom God created not as isolated atoms, but as complex social beings.

On the other hand, Trent had also underlined the fact that sound doctrine could not make its impact felt without a practical savvy displaying cognizance of the changeability of earthly conditions. Achieving Christ's sovereignty over the world demanded a recognition that the application of Catholic teaching at any time in history was in no way a straightforward mechanical process, much less an easy one. "Feeding the sheep" always entailed insightful pastoral nuance, combining acceptance of the fact that the basic strength of the Church lies in her supernatural message and the grace that she offers for the transformation of nature with an acute awareness of the particular concrete problems of securing the victory of the Catholic position in any given historical situation.

Pastoral occupation of the" spaces of social life" was especially difficult in a Western world that had been converted to the Enlightenment naturalist spirit in a highly patchy manner. This conversion had not taken place in a completely hostile fashion. Rather, it had often involved a *cooption* of aspects of Christian ideas and Christian inspired institutions in support of quite contradictory secularist positions—as our nineteenth century thinkers recognized had indeed happened in the Catholic world in the 1700s. Moreover, there remained "social spaces" in Enlightenment conquered territory still subject to the continued, though weakened, influence of solid religious beliefs and authorities.

All this guaranteed that the contemporary West was a "mixed bag". Purification of its confusing elements required a demanding surgical operation carried out in a way that removed "modernity" as a dominant and destructive ideology from the merely "modern" aspects of the social body. The potential value of what was merely modern could then be confirmed, purified of its fallen flaws, and transformed for the greater glory of God and the secular benefit of society. In performing their earthly tasks properly, the manifold purified authorities of a complex society would then also work effectively to raise individuals to the appreciation of things divine and fulfillment of the divine plan. What was left from contemporary life — the infection of modernity — could at that point happily be isolated and tossed onto the rubbish heap of history.

CHAPTER 2

Dangers on the Purification Front

UNFORTUNATELY FOR CATHOLICS, THE Church's quest for purification of the spaces of public life in 1918 was a hotly contested one, with her Gnostic, Nominalist, Reformation, and Enlightenment shaped opponents either potentially or immediately wielding more power than she might ever hope to command on her own. Dangers on the purification front were international, national, and broadly cultural in character, with most of the threats in question ultimately perilous on all these levels. *La Civiltà Cattolica* continued to apply and develop the conclusions reached by the revival movement of the previous century to understand and parry them. Therefore, much of what I have to say below is fit into the broad framework that this journal's interwar analysis provided.

One of the two newer — but historically rooted — perils of the interwar period emerged from the United States. Due to her entry into the European conflict, and President Woodrow Wilson's statement of allied goals in his Fourteen Points, his response to Pope Benedict XV's peace proposals, and his popularization of the worldwide struggle as "the war to end all wars", America loomed large as a potential purifying influence on November 11th, 1918 and in the months thereafter. Although the rejection of the Treaty of Versailles by the United States Senate and her consequent failure to participate in the League of Nations removed the imminent threat of New World competition for the *political* control of spaces in the Old, America's "isolationism" in the interwar years was never truly complete. Latin America and East Asia remained public American concerns and fields of action, and New World *cultural* impact — the American way of life — also continued to grow unabated in much of Europe as well. Cultural "Americanism" eased the way to American political domination of the European world in the wake of the second global conflagration. By 1945, mobilization of the American Way — what then came to be called pluralism — as a weapon for coaxing the reawakened Catholic Faith of the nineteenth and early twentieth centuries back into its eighteenth century dogmatic slumber was complete.

A second new force competing with the Church for the occupation and purification of social spaces came out of Russia, which, although it played no role as a nation at the Paris Peace Conference in 1919, was nevertheless "present" in everyone's mind at that gathering. For the seizure of power in Russia by Lenin's Bolsheviks — formally known as the Communist Party from March, 1918 onwards — and the impact that Marxism-Leninism immediately exercised outside that troubled country's fluctuating borders gave grave significance the world over to what was happening therein. This was certainly true in the defeated nations, Germany's Communist movement sparking the Spartacist uprising of the weeks preceding the opening of the Peace Conference, and Hungary experiencing a Soviet style government briefly thereafter. But the spirit of the Revolution was not unknown to the victors either, with Red Guards seizing factories and agricultural estates and dreaming of an Italian imitation of the distant Russian model.

Naturalist competition for the occupation of the spaces of life in the interwar world also came from more familiar liberal and liberal democratic victims of the Western illness. These were represented by the existing governments of the core powers of the Entente Alliance who ultimately subscribed to the treaties coming out of the Paris Peace Conference: France, Britain, and Italy. Still bound, publically, to Wilson's millenarian rhetoric, the victorious Entente states could not avoid working through the League of Nations whose creation he had championed, shoring up its weaknesses through a policy of Great Power "collective security" supposedly assuring Europe and the world the eternal peace that the American president had promised. The mockery, in practice, of the hopes for a purification represented by a peace guided according to the pure will of the victors and their more familiar liberal manifestation of the Western disease was very much emphasized by the *Civiltà* editors. Hence, they criticized the Paris Peace Settlement as doing nothing other than bringing all the influences of the European liberal interpretation of the Gnostic-Nominalist Reformation-Enlightenment order of things that the journal had already outlined in 1850 to their logical conclusions.[1]

What did this entail? To begin with, it meant a continued heyday for the materialist, parochial-minded, liberal-approved form of nationalism that still dominated the worldview of the victors. Diseased national feeling was said to be obvious in the vindictive injustices inflicted upon Germany, Austria, and Hungary in the three treaties dealing with them that came out of the Paris Peace Conference; injustices reaching their peak with the occupation of the Ruhr region in 1923, brought about by German failure to pay the exorbitant reparations demanded of that economically shattered and psychologically demoralized country. Moreover, the imperialism this unjust nationalism generated was worsened after the war by the expansion of colonialism throughout the carcass of the Ottoman Empire; something that particularly concerned the Church with respect to the British opening of Palestine to Zionist

---

[1] See J. Rao, "Catholicism, Liberalism, and the Right: a Sketch from the 1920s", http://jcrao.freeshell.org/CatholicismandtheRight.html. Much of the following is also taken from J. Rao, *Black Legends and the Light of the World* (Remnant Press, 2012), pp. 504–562. Only direct citations are footnoted.

migration and what this might mean for the ultimate fate of the holy city of Jerusalem. Finally, power in the hands of a "League of Nations" with no serious roots in European society, simply ensured the organization's manipulation at the hands of the victorious allies—or, rather, whoever it was that controlled their governments internally.

Speculation regarding the real powers behind the throne brings us to the *Civiltà's* unchanging emphasis upon the basic consequences of the evisceration of legitimate social authorities, already begun by the secularizing "absolutist" monarchies of the pre-revolutionary world, and then carried forward more successfully by Enlightenment liberalism under the claim that such surgery was necessary to "free" the individual from tyranny. What this emasculation of authority had actually guaranteed was not the liberation of all but, rather, the empowering of the stronger and better-organized bullies of any given country to manipulate their fellow-citizens in the social vacuum thus created.

Incited by a given passion—and liberalism potentially blessed and divinized them all—partisan groups rushed for control of the arms of the weakened liberal State, insisting that it was transmitting into action the "will of the people" for an unquestionable good. A State directed by the "will of the people", as interpreted by the liberating faction actually seizing power, then proceeded to destroy all remaining non-governmental social authorities that were hostile to its desires. Since potential private usurpers of the functions of the weakened liberal State were legion—capitalists, the press, unions, gangs of armed soldiers or vigilantes, libertines, and madmen of every stripe—the hostile authorities destroyed must eventually lead to the disarmament of all surviving social institutions. Hence, the liberal project ends with the individual confronting an oligarchic party controlling a supposedly weak State which now, in practice, is made capable of doing whatsoever pleases the faction in question: in the name of "The People", although against the population's own true will. "Everything", the *Civiltà* wrote at the beginning of the interwar era, "has been obscured and overturned due to the lack of a social sense, in order to serve the triumph of individual and collective egoisms".[2]

Financial magnates, the journal argued, were still the real oligarchic powers behind the throne of the victors at the time of the Paris Peace Conference. Atomistic liberalism, justifying an individualism which sinful men quite eagerly aimed towards obtaining property for the satisfaction of material desires, had provided the capitalist with his ticket to a destructive journey across the nineteenth-century Europe. The weakened State had collapsed before his excessive desires and therefore became his ideological tool. Justice, to the capitalist, was nothing but the assurance that the defenseless and the unambitious received no protection from his exorbitant demands. And it was not just the European continent that was littered with the results of his wrong-headed "freedom", but also its global colonial empires and Wilson's proto-Pluralist America.

Catholic counter-revolutionaries had a long history of viewing militant socialism as a providential scourge for capitalism's indifference to human suffering. Given this history of injustice, *La Civiltà Cattolica* was not surprised that liberal economic freedom had also engendered support for a militant, revolutionary, Marxism-Leninism. Yes, this movement might in one way seem to be a purely cerebral one, in that it, like all Marxist exponents, saw the emergence of the final communist stage of history as an inevitability. Nevertheless, its sense that the birth of this «end time» involved a purification of the bourgeois decadence that was the accompaniment of the penultimate phase of man's experience on the earth, and its cultivation of an elite party as the righteous torchbearer of a welcome purifying fire, demonstrated its share in the particular quest characterizing the particular age and place we are discussing.

[2] Rao, "A Sketch", note 7.

But reaction to an internal power vacuum filled first by liberal capitalists and now threatened by a Soviet-focused, international communism was to bring up one other materialist, passionate, irrational competitor for occupation and purification of the spaces of life: fascism. Born in a victorious but severely troubled liberal Italy, this new phenomenon was essentially shaped by Benito Mussolini's (1883–1945) recognition of the bonding of frontline soldiers with one another under obedience to the orders of officers who shared their sufferings in an "egalitarian" way in the trenches. It was the vision of what the transfer of self-sacrificing, energetic, manly action in subordination to a "comrade-leader" from the trenches to the peacetime world might achieve in the way of purifying the nation and solidifying national unity that really gave the movement its strength.

And it was this same vision that fueled the creation of fascist parties throughout the world, each of them adding local variations to what was deemed essential for the purification of the country concerned properly to take effect. In Spain, this engendered the call by the Falange for purification through a worldwide revival of pride in the Hispanic achievement. In Germany, it entailed National Socialism's insistence upon a purification of a biological nature, with racial cleansing as the necessary foundation for a fruitful national community—a *Volksgemeinschaft*—all of whose elements might then work democratically "in gear" with one another—*Gleichschaltung*—in obedience to the will of the comrade-leader.

Interwar Europe, faced as it was with a variety of irrational, willful partisan forces, all the hatreds that their clash had to engender or intensify, and a multiplicity of projects for purification of the Western disease was, in the *Civiltà's* mind, a disaster waiting to happen — "and please God that a new and more profound destruction does not take place".[3] Alas, that destruction appeared to the editors

---

[3] Rao, "A Sketch", note 2.

to be more than likely. "We foresee more ferocious warfare", they lamented as the Paris Peace Settlement went into effect, "more difficult conditions for the good, a more menacing future for society as a whole".[4]

---

[4] Rao, "A Sketch", note 2

CHAPTER 3

Purification and Doctrine in the Interwar Era

INSISTENCE ON A PURIFICATION ACHIEVED through submission of the natural to the supernatural world, taught by the nineteenth century Catholic revival movement and vigorously supported by the Papacy since the time of Pius IX (1846–1878), very clearly still characterized the teaching, in encyclicals, allocutions, and letters to individual bishops and episcopacies, of the two quite different popes of the bulk of the interwar period: Benedict XV (1914–1922) and Pius XI (1922–1939). Both placed emphasis upon doctrines and devotions that well illustrated how nature was purified through connection with the supernatural, perhaps most significantly with reference to those concerning the Sacred Heart of Jesus, as in Pius XI's *Miserentissimus Redemptor* (1928) and *Caritate Christi compulsi* (1932). A lasting postwar purification, this same pontiff declared in *Ubi arcano Dei consilio* (1922), was only possible by ensuring the peace of Christ in the reign of Christ.

Purification, in the minds of the nineteenth century protagonists of Catholic revival, was intellectually very much dependent upon a deeper ecclesiology, one that truly understood the Roman Catholic Church as the Mystical Body and the fullness of her role as such in transforming the world in Christ. The earlier historical development of Catholic ecclesiology had been interrupted because of the politicization of the Papacy and the influence of an anti-speculative, philosophical and theological Nominalism from the thirteenth century onwards. Serious progress was only begun again at Trent, but here, too, had still been severely hampered due to the opposition of regalist States demanding firm control of their "national" churches. The First Vatican Council's much more serious labors in the ecclesiological realm were also halted in the face of numerous factors, theological and political, so that what was accomplished under its aegis proved tragically incomplete.

Nevertheless, ultramontanist pressure at Vatican One ensured the definition of the doctrine of Papal Infallibility, thereby greatly strengthening the position of the Holy See in the life of the Universal Church. This stronger influence was reflected in the new code of Canon Law of 1917 (*Providentissimus Mater*) and took yet further practical shape in the interwar era. A "papal" outlook was encouraged through the clerical elite formed at the various national and specialized colleges of the Eternal City, which then transmitted the Roman message back to their homes. Certain prelates, men like William Henry Cardinal O'Connell (1859–1944), the Archbishop of Boston (1907–1944), were looked upon by many as serving as something akin to papal "viceroys" in their specific countries. This ultramontane exaltation of the Holy See was further confirmed through the canonization of saints known for their commitment to Rome, such as Robert Bellarmine (1930) and two of the English martyrs, John Fisher and Thomas More (both in 1935). It was therefore a much more self-confident Papacy, certain that the Roman Church held the key to the purification of a troubled world, that rejected, in *Mortalium animos* (1928), the appeal for an ecumenical Christian effort to purify the globe made by men such as Charles Brent (1862–1929), Episcopal Missionary Bishop of the Philippine Islands and Nathan Söderblom (1866–1931), the Archbishop of Uppsala, at such postwar gatherings as that at Oud Wassenaar in the Netherlands in 1919.

Mobilization of all intellectual forces to aid in teaching the doctrines of the Incarnation, the Mystical Body, and Christ as King of a purified universe flowed from the very nature of the concepts involved. In philosophical terms, Rome continued to argue that good teaching required offering of pride of place to the Thomist revival officially promoted by the Church since the pontificate of Leo XIII. Both the encyclical *Studiorum Ducem*, issued in the context of the general celebration of the six hundredth anniversary of the canonization of St. Thomas Aquinas in 1923, as well as the canonization of Albertus Magnus in 1931, helped to make this Roman commitment clear. Men like Reginald Garrigou-Lagrange (1877–1964), Antonin-Gilbert Sertillanges (1863–1948), Jacques Maritain (1882–1973), Etienne Gilson (1884–1978), and, on the popular level, G.K. Chesterton (1874–1936), all contributed to the interwar era's reputation as a great age of Catholic Neo-Thomism.

Nevertheless, the reigns of Benedict XV and Pius XI allowed much more scope for the expression and mobilization of non-Thomist theological and philosophical schools of thought as well. While never condemned as such under Pope St. Pius X, these other approaches had indeed been treated as *ipso facto* suspect at the height of the anti-Modernist campaign. An easing of tensions permitted further opportunity for the teachings of Soren Kierkegaard (1813–1855), Edmund Husserl (1859–1938), and Max Scheler (1874–1928) to find their way into the work of phenomenologists like Gabriel Marcel (1889–1973) and Dietrich von Hildebrand (1889–1977). Those of Henri Bergson (1859–1941) had an impact even upon such passionately Thomist thinkers as Maritain.

Positive theology, which had also fallen into the shadows under Pope St. Pius X, was another beneficiary of the change of atmosphere. The influence of the biblical criticism of Fr. Marie-Joseph Lagrange (1855–1938) and his students took firmer root. The last volume of Ludwig von Pastor's (1855–1928) *History of the Papacy* was published in 1930, with further critical work being done by Christopher Dawson (1889–1970), the young Henri Daniel-Rops (1901–1965), and, once again on the popular level, by men like

Chesterton and his compatriot, Hilaire Belloc (1870–1953). Agostino Gemelli, O.F.M. (1878–1959), a psychologist, was instrumental in founding the Catholic University of the Sacred Heart of Milan (1921) for the broad education of Catholic men and women.

Speculative and positive theological studies were given official organizational backing in Rome. The Dominican dominated Angelicum, where Garrigou-Lagrange taught from 1909–1960, was the key Thomist center. A "Gregorian Consortium", created by the Jesuits in 1930, combined the original institution bearing that name together with the Biblicum, established in 1907, and the Oriental Institute, founded in 1917, wherein the influence of Eugene Tisserant (1884–1972), another student of Lagrange, was to become significant. The Gregorian of the interwar years expanded the scope of its work, missiology (1932) becoming one of the additions most pregnant with consequences, as will be seen below. Meanwhile, an already existing scientific institution was transformed in 1936 into the Pontifical Academy of Sciences and placed under the leadership of Gemelli, with eleven Nobel Prize winners among the early members.

These intellectual forces then, in turn, worked to validate and stimulate human effort to enlist each and every natural element to play its role in God's redemptive — and purifying — plan. No Marxist Antonio Gramsci (1891–1937) was needed to convince the contemporary Roman Catholic Church intellectually just how much occupation of the "spaces" of culture in general — that of the masses as well as of the elite — was essential to a victory over society at large. Roman concern for artistic matters was reflected in papal addresses of various kinds, focusing on the newer cultural problems of mass sport, radio, and the cinema, along with those of more venerable character. The Pontifical Academy of Fine Arts and Letters of the Virtuosi of the Pantheon, another old establishment given new life by Pius XI in 1928, sought to encourage architects, painters, filmmakers, sculptors, academicians of art and music, poets, and novelists alike. This grasp of the importance of control of the culture was also very much reflected in the interwar period in the extremely perceptive commentaries of the contemporary Portuguese Catholic economist, statesman, and general social critic, Antonio Oliveira de Salazar (1889–1970). And, needless to say, interwar Europe did indeed witness a flowering of Catholic activity in manifold cultural spheres.

Intense spiritual reinforcement was given to the Catholic teaching of the need for a purification of all the spaces of life obtainable only through nature's recognition of its dependency upon the supernatural. Perhaps most symbolic in this regard was the establishment of the Feast of Christ the King through *Quas primas* (1925). The four canonizations completed under Pope Benedict and the twenty-one of Pius XI all emphasized the role of Mary and the saints in grasping or reflecting the consequences of the natural-supernatural union made palpable by the Incarnation. Hence, the canonizations associated with saintly devotion to the Sacred Heart, such as those of Margaret Mary Alacoque (1920) and John Eudes (1925), or with Mary as the conduit for the "health" of the world in general—as seen through the raising to the altar of Bernadette Soubirou (1926) and recognition of the "purifying" significance of the grotto at Lourdes. It is instructive to note in this regard that Pius XI viewed the canonization of Thérèse of the Child Jesus and the Holy Face, Thérèse of Lisieux (1925), the saint most linked with the offering up of all the smallest aspects of life *ad majorem Dei gloriam*, as the star of his pontificate.

International congresses promoting a deeper understanding of the Eucharist and its liturgical context were another powerful interwar spiritual tool. These were held the globe over: in Rome (1922), Amsterdam (1924), Chicago (1926), Sydney (1928), Carthage (1930), Dublin (1932), Buenos Aires (1934), Manila (1934), and Budapest (1938). Eucharistic congresses not only served as a spur to practical personal sanctification, but also, through the purification of the individual, to the proper functioning of social institutions, ecclesiastical and secular alike. For it was only by means of men and women awakened to their need to transform themselves in Christ through the Eucharist that the world could be given the authorities of Church, State, and society at large capable of carrying out their purifying missions in a truthful, virtuous, Christian manner.

Nineteenth century theorists deeply concerned with this purification of the social order as a whole retained Trent's conviction that practical labor be rooted in sound doctrinal principles. Such work had to be preceded by a clear understanding of what the Faith sought to achieve through the occupation of public spaces; what they labeled the Catholic "thesis". Given the character of the Church's central mission, the Catholic "thesis" had to emphasize the primacy of the spirit, and "the spiritual, above all else" could easily be viewed as the motto of the Papacy in the interwar period.

Pius XI was deeply disturbed by Catholic temptations to succumb to pressures to subordinate the spiritual to natural guidelines. This temptation was impressed upon him before becoming Pope, when, as Nuncio to the newly restored Poland, he was told by the local episcopacy that it required no theological "update" after all the years of subjection to non-Catholic rule, since a proper understanding of the Faith was already guaranteed by mere possession of the "national soul". Such a statement was redolent of the error of the Abbé de Lamennais (1782–1854), condemned in the previous century, which taught that the sense of the Faith, and therefore the guide to understanding its teaching, was something emerging from the natural endowment of Catholic Peoples themselves—in effect, aside from and potentially in opposition to the supernatural magisterium of the bishops and the pope. Pius XI was vehement in his insistence that Catholics active in the political and social realm accept the primacy of the supernatural revelation and avoid this and other inversions of the hierarchy of values, tantamount to proclaiming what was essentially natural as the key to things spiritual.

Still, a basically spiritual Catholic "thesis", was nevertheless rooted in the reality that the supernatural had been linked with nature in a new way through God becoming man. This meant that the supra-rational truth of the Incarnation, the fact that God had confirmed the validity of a natural world which nevertheless had to be redeemed and corrected of its flaws, had practical consequences which the Catholic purifier of the social order was obliged, doctrinally, to take into account in his work.

The first of these was that both the knowledge of the specific natural character of any aspect of life as well as its subjection to the supernatural tools of correction and transformation were essential to Catholic Action. Hence, to take but one example, the natural functioning and "laws" of economic life must be treated seriously, but always with a recognition of their human and sinful limitations and need to be subordinated to the supernatural laws of justice and charity. The natural and the supernatural must be made to work together simultaneously.

Secondly, just as the Incarnation and the creation of the Mystical Body taught that the individual can only be purified through membership in and obedience to Christ and His Church, their message for all of man's earthly activity underlined the truth that individuals are meant to work on the natural plane as social beings, through societies, under the guidance of social authorities. The individual is perfected naturally and aimed upwards towards the worship of God not as an isolated atom, but through social institutions, whose purpose is fulfilled insofar as they recognize that this perfecting and uplifting labor is their raison d'être.

The need for the Catholic to treat as doctrine the spiritually rooted "thesis" insisting upon the value and harmony of all things natural and supernatural, individual and social, as the basis for every aspect of human life and action was stressed throughout the interwar period, as in the encyclicals on education (*Divini illius Magistri*, 1929), on the family (*Casti connubii*, 1930), and on economics

(*Quadragesimo anno*, 1931). A doctrinal need to reject as unacceptable any modern ideology that denied the primacy of the spiritual, the validity and harmony of things earthly and supernatural, and the need of the individual to be subject to social authorities which understood their mission to be that of the perfection of the human person according to both natural and divine law was also made clear. Hence, the condemnations of an economically materialist communism in *Acerba Anima* (1932), *Dilectissima nobis* (1933), and *Divini Redemptoris* (1937) and a racially materialist National Socialist in *Mit Brennender Sorge* (1937), both of these forces fundamentally subordinating the spirit to nature, and in ways that were destructive to the dignity of each individual body and soul. Rome's doctrinal trenches in an interwar period that manifested dangers on all fronts might, therefore, be viewed, as though they were well manned and well maintained. Commitment to the "thesis" seemed to be assured.

CHAPTER 4

Practical Questions and a Quest for Purification Gone Mad

A. THE CATHOLIC "THESIS" AND ITS "HYPOTHETICAL" DILEMMAS

CATHOLICS IN 1918 HAD AVAILABLE TO them a treasure trove of practical speculations from nineteenth and early twentieth century activists regarding how to put the "thesis" into practice. Here one could find highly specific suggestions regarding how to work with, but correct, the moral and structural flaws of the existing socio-political order. But one also encountered a variety of plans for the complete replacement of what many called the "established disorder" by what was referred to as a "corporate society".

Corporatists of Catholic mettle envisaged the creation of a modern version of what they argued was organically developing in the Middle Ages: a society composed of many diverse societies, all of whose authorities worked to aid the individual, both on the earthly and supernatural level, under the ultimate direction of Church and State. Among those Catholics who continued to promote corporatism in the 1920s and 1930s were the Portuguese economist and Prime Minister, Antonio de Oliveira Salazar, identified above for his broad achievement as a social and cultural critic, the ex-soldier and Austrian Chancellor, Engelbert Dollfuss (1892–1934), and the editor of the newspaper that the chancellor funded, *Der Christliche*

Ständestaat, the phenomenologist Dietrich von Hildebrand. Salazar very clearly understood the need for a proper Christian international order to stand guarantor for the success of the Catholic "thesis" in any given European country. Due to Austria's peculiar and precarious interwar situation, Dollfuss was also very eager to stress the need for a victory of Catholic principles of international law to ensure the survival of the "German, Christian, corporate State" he envisaged.

Reformers of the existing socio-political order were convinced that modern though this might be, it did not have to be considered hopelessly corrupted by the spirit of modernity. They believed that a separation of the chaff from the wheat could be made. Meanwhile, corporatists rejected arguments that their "thesis" was hopelessly "nostalgic" in character, since they insisted that it was based upon the very nature of things, adjustable, in practice, from age to age, in the ways they sought to identify. And both could make a case that their particular approaches were justified by papal documents relating the Catholic "thesis" to practical matters, such as *Quadragesimo anno* with respect to economics.

Attempting a practical Catholic purification of the social order based upon sound doctrine has obviously always been a daunting enterprise. This is true even when such a labor has been undertaken in societies openly confessing the Faith. After all, such societies may publicly pay their respects to the Church's teachings and the primacy of the spirit in human life, but nevertheless still ignore, do damage to, and even totally subvert Catholic doctrine in practice. Human fallibility, compounded by the sinfulness of the spiritual and political heads of Catholic Christendom as well as her ordinary members, make these dangers a constant threat. Pastoral success in a fallen world requires possession not just of the words of the Faith, but also a deep sense of humility, tact, the wisdom of serpents, and a day-to-day tenacity gained only through confession, communion, fasting, and prayer.

Moreover, maintenance of a purified social order requires an apostolic spirit further demanding that the existing Christian community not "stand pat". That spirit calls for an effort to go beyond the status quo to evangelize disbelievers and purify the societies *they* control. If Catholics do not respond to this call for further apostolic effort, they fail to live up to the Gospel message and jeopardize the security of societies which at least on the surface appear already to have been won to Christ, making them smug in their Catholicism and perilously indifferent to the continued impact of the disbelieving outside world upon them.

Throughout Church History, this evangelization of the non-Catholic world has involved the taking of serious risks that might or might not be successful; risks whose mistakes could only be handled through maintenance of a truly self-critical attitude on the part of believers prepared to entertain objections to their decisions and correction of them; risks taking into account the peculiar conditions of their time and place. Wise and humble Church authorities, evangelists, and socio-political activists eager to make judgments regarding how Catholics should work practically and effectively to purify the interwar European world had to understand the real conditions of their own time that made the attainment of the "thesis" difficult and perhaps even temporarily impossible: what their nineteenth century forbears labeled the "hypothesis". Consideration of the hypothesis in the years 1918–1939 involved distinguishing among four different kinds of contemporary influences: three of them, while significantly diverse, nevertheless offering a common problem for the "official" Catholic position in what might be called a "soft" or seemingly friendly manner; the fourth, "hard" influence being openly and aggressively hostile to purification in the Catholic manner.

A first "softly" problematic force encompasses a number of monarchist and army-guided movements that publically argued in favor of a central role for the Roman Catholic Church in social life.

These sometimes cooperated with one another, as in the case of the Spanish Civil War (1936–1939). The "soft" force that counted the most in terms of its intellectual influence was the *Action Française* of Charles Maurras (1868–1952), which taught the need to build a strong France on the basis of its identifiably constructive historic elements: the legitimate monarchy, Catholicism, a socio-political decentralization evoking much corporatist thought, and the beneficent influence of Greco-Roman culture.

A second "soft" problem must be introduced with reference to a serious cultural dilemma; that offered by the many immensely gifted and vocal men and women deeply marked by the war experience. Seeing the world around them turned upside down, such "burned" Westerners became seekers, looking for a way out that often led them to a rediscovery of the Catholic past. Nevertheless, this rediscovery was frequently mingled together with an exploration of the esoteric aspects of Western cultural history, a fascination with modern literary and artistic iconoclasm, an enthusiasm for exotic ideas and practices from Africa, Asia, the Caribbean, and Indian Latin America, and sundry baggage from their personal past, including that coming from their varied frontline war experiences. Unfortunately, these other elements, often shorn of any "seeker" interest in or even accompanied by an open contempt for the Faith, very much remained a foundation for the cultural work of other talented but anti-Christian men and women of the era.

Still, there is no denying the emergence from among the seekers of men of profoundly Christian moral and mystical feeling cultivating undeniably modern and esoteric interests and style, such as T.S. Eliot (1888–1965); of slowly evolving writers like Ernst Jünger, who moved from glorifying the purification that came from the cult of irrational violence in his early works to a militant defense of things truly rooted in nature in a strange but beautiful novel-allegory, *Auf den Marmorklippen* (*On the Marble Cliffs*, 1939); or of men of letters similar to Josef Roth (1894–1939), who longed deeply for the restoration of the order of the old "sacred" Austrian Empire, and is said to have asked for a Catholic funeral alongside his Jewish one.

Mention of Roth cannot help but call up a further reference to his fellow Jew and former compatriot, the multifaceted Karl Kraus (1874–1936), editor of a Viennese journal called *Die Fackel* (*The Torch*). Kraus, a master of venomous ridicule, shared almost all the criticisms of the modern world — if not necessarily the key to correcting them — enunciated by the editors of *La Civiltà Cattolica*. He, too, was convinced that he was living in the barbaric "last days of mankind", where "hell reigns"; a world which, while moving inexorably towards a new war, could only truly be purified (echoing Jünger) by getting "back to the basics". As the composer Ernst Krenek relates:[1]

> At a time when people were generally decrying the Japanese bombardment of Shanghai, I met Karl Kraus struggling over one of his famous comma problems. He said something like: 'I know that everything is futile when the house is burning. But I have to do this as long as it is at all possible; for if those who were supposed to look after commas had always made sure they were in the right place, Shanghai would not be burning.

Separating out the valid use of things modern and the study of diverse natural ways of presenting eternal truths from acceptance of the ideology of modernity or an uncritical plunge into the nostalgic or the esoteric was an awkward enterprise on the cultural plane. These same difficulties were paralleled politically by the problem of dealing with liberals and liberal governments "burned" by the disillusionments of the war, and now often seemingly ready to contemplate listening to what Catholics had to say

[1] Hans Weigel, *Kraus: Die Macht der Ohnmacht* (Brandstätter, 1986), p. 128

in a more open way. The existence of a group of more friendly liberals was a fact of life in the interwar period, but complications in responding to their apparent change of heart emerged from their expectation that the Church should be "reasonable" and modify her own position in exchange. Sharing certain common enemies with her, these friendlier liberals wished to use her influence to combat their joint foes, and either misunderstood or feigned belief in the ease of gaining friendship with Catholics to win her help. Some fascists in various countries also become part of this camp, and for precisely the same reasons.

A related and final "soft" problem came from the ambiguously "isolationist" United States. This was a nation very much shaped by the English Whig experience that was also instrumental in giving birth to European liberalism in general. "Americanism" argued that its own particular liberal constitutional system had become "the last, best hope of mankind", providing everyone enjoying its blessings the greatest freedom ever known in history. Many American Catholics, believing this claim, then insisted that the nation's commitment to "freedom" offered the best possible chance for an institution like the Roman Church to thrive, unmolested, to fulfill her mission; that the liberty characterizing their country was far more likely to bring about the triumph of the Faith than any traditional union of Church and State.

While indeed distinct, these three forces are at times hard to distinguish in terms of the practical dilemmas they create for a Catholic purification of society. While seeking an alliance, they continued to praise ideas or pursue policies which were anti-Catholic, and which they apparently expected the Church to ignore lest the battle against "the real threat" to purification of the social order should profit by their open disagreement. The most basic error in their position from the standpoint of the Catholic "thesis" was their primary emphasis not upon spiritual questions but on political systems and politics in general: *politique d'abord*, "politics first", in the words of Charles Maurras. Interwar Catholic authorities and activists open to the "hypothesis" would have had to combine a response to their friendly embrace with the maintenance of a certain distance from their grip, recognizing that an uncritical alliance with them could easily lead to their own seduction, and the gradual abandonment of the fullness of the "thesis". But the temptation on the part of Catholics to give themselves over, heart and soul, to what such "soft" forces wished was increased by the fear on the part of believers of actually doing what their potential "ally" repeatedly claimed any open chastisement of their flaws would ensure: namely, guaranteeing the victory of whatever was identified as "the greater evil".

Finally, interwar Church authorities and Catholic activists dealing with the "hypothesis" would have had to admit that the era in which they lived was filled with men and governments utterly and openly contemptuous of the Church and in no way interested even in manipulating her for their own purposes. The clear goal of communists, many fascists, a good number of old-line liberals, and others too varied to mention was the outright destruction of the Faith.

But here, too, dilemmas arose, for these open enemies of Christ were, after all, still natural human beings, and sometimes represented understandable reactions to previous flaws and injustices. They awakened in a number of fervent Catholics a laudable concern for their conversion. Such evangelists of the open enemy argued that the Church especially had to understand the reasons why ideas and movements seemingly closed to the message of Redemption had proven capable of obtaining such mass appeal and political power. She had to do so, they insisted, if only for the purpose of developing a pastoral strategy that would either counter their dangerous influence or demonstrate to them that any valid hopes for purification that they nurtured could only be fulfilled through the message of Catholic Christianity.

B. THE "PARTIES OF ORDER" AND PRACTICAL CATHOLIC FAILURES IN THE INTERWAR PERIOD

Even if we presume that the best of Catholic wills lay behind the practical decisions taken to purify the "hypothesis" represented by the interwar world, I believe that their overall quality was sorely deficient. Unfortunate mistakes of terrible consequence were made by Church authorities and lay Catholic political forces. Moreover, a current of thought promoting an abandonment of the vision of the nineteenth century revival movement and departing from the simultaneously doctrinal-pastoral pathway to purification so properly stressed by the Council of Trent matured throughout the years in question. This new vision of Christian order came to full fruition in the political and social climate presided over by the victors of the Second World War and through the strange work of the Second Vatican Council.

I do not think that criticism of the mistakes of the interwar era should focus upon supra national affairs. Rome did what she could with the international community, friendly or hostile as it might be, without backtracking on the teachings of the Catholic Faith. While theoretically critical of the Paris Peace Settlement as a whole, the papal court worked openly to lessen the vindictiveness of the victors in a truly Christian manner. It encouraged the reintegration of Germany into European life signaled by the Locarno Pact of 1925, along with Aristide Briand's further initiatives for Franco-German reconciliation and world peace, seeing in them an opportunity to make of collective security a truly just enterprise and the League of Nations a more credible force for the global common good.

Alas, men like Antonio de Oliveira Salazar and Engelbert Dollfuss were well aware that everything that physically weak countries — such as their own — and physically frail institutions — like the Roman Church — ultimately believed and hoped to achieve remained totally dependent upon what the Great Powers decided to do. Great Power decisions were in turn based upon their own internal situations. It was "locally" that the fate of the international community, both in Europe and the world at large, would be determined. Let us therefore undertake our critique of the flawed Catholic strategy for purification on precisely this level, and begin to do so by giving greater flesh to the "hypothesis" faced by Catholics in the interwar period on the national level.

Enlightenment-minded liberals, always terrified by the "demagogic" consequences of democracy, expected a postwar Europe dominated by universal manhood suffrage to result in governments of a Catholic or socialist character, both of them deemed disastrous for the materialist, individual economic freedom they cherished. 1918 saw them very much on the lookout for some means of defusing this seemingly inevitable but unwanted victory. Non-liberal but also non-Catholic and non-socialist rightist forces, including the army leadership of certain countries, as well as irregular bands of both returning soldiers and civilians upset by civil disorder in their home countries, were equally unhappy with the possible radicalizing consequences of democratic changes.

The Bolshevik Revolution in Russia in 1917 and its potential spread through fellow travelers in Germany, Austria, Hungary, Italy, and elsewhere from 1918 onwards offered a way out of the dilemma. Liberals and the rightists in question, to which the budding fascist movements in Italy and Germany can also be added, were openly anti-Bolshevik. But so were Catholics and other religious minded counter-revolutionaries. Moreover, they were joined in this hostility by the mainline socialist movement, angered by the fact that the Bolshevik victory had split the International in two, with a significant minority abandoning commitment to democratic politics to follow the Marxist-Leninists in their support of a militant, dictatorial party as the agent of revolutionary change.

Two "Party of Order" camps — in many ways reminiscent of the French movement initially using this term to create an alliance to oppose the first practical appearance of Socialism as a political force in Paris in 1848 — thus quickly came into being after the war's end to fight the communist menace, with each of them making an appeal for Catholic support. One of these operated through liberal democracy, even if all of its supporting elements did not necessarily approve of liberalism or democratic institutions, as was the case with the German General Staff in its backing of the anti-communist but basically liberal-Catholic-socialist run Weimar Republic. The other was authoritarian in its structures, even if not necessarily anti-democratic in spirit, and often aided by many liberals, due, above all else, to its perceived friendliness to their private property interests. There were many variations of this second Party of Order camp, often army dominated, but frequently after 1922 being seen as having its best chance for success through some kind of imitation of Italian fascism.

These two camps achieved a certain stability that nevertheless was sometimes threatened in the 1920s due to internal factors in one country or another. Stability was then much more broadly menaced after 1929 as a result of the Great Depression, the apparent inability of liberal capitalism to deal with its ravages, and the renewed influence for communism, unleashed by the enthusiasm surrounding the first Soviet Five Year Plan, fed by the propaganda of the Comintern and its fellow travelers.

A rebirth of European-wide instability resulted in a pronounced tilt in the direction of the authoritarian Party of Order camp, with new fascist and army victories in many places. In Germany, the army leadership, convinced that liberal democracy could no longer stave off the communist menace, threw its support to Hitler's National Socialist movement. From the death of President von Hindenburg in 1934, the Führer, backed by the armed forces, was totally free to mobilize all aspects of life to work democratically "in gear" with one another (*Gleischschaltung*), and to erect the racial community (*Volksgemeinschaft*) considered essential for social purification. National Socialists, fascists, army-led forces, or other authoritarian representatives of this Party of Order camp, whether successful as in Spain after its bitter Civil War, or merely hoping to gain power as in France throughout the 1920s and 1930s, all, in different ways, continued to appeal to Catholics for support against the greater communist evil.

But who was it, politically, that would be the mouthpiece for the Catholic response? One possibility was the network of Catholic political parties, Catholic lobbies, and Catholic unions that had been created in the latter part of the nineteenth century to defend the "thesis" from hostile attacks and to work for social justice as the Church understood it. The German world and the Lowlands had played a central role in developing this network, and the Catholic parties of Germany, Austria, Belgium, and the Netherlands were still powerful forces in the interwar era. But before addressing their labors from 1918–1939, we must first note that they had to contend with powerful inner-Catholic difficulties, beginning with those offered by the highest authorities of the Church.

For Rome was not fond of much of this existing network of basically lay organizations with broad political and social goals. The Holy See did not like the idea of political parties calling themselves "Catholic" and appealing to believers under such a title. It appreciated it even less when clerics were involved in party activities, thereby taking time and energy away from their spiritual role. The Papacy saw the institutional Church as the only force that could legitimately use the Catholic name, because she alone could vouch for the doctrinal accuracy of the path to purification being taken. On the one hand, Rome felt that political parties, especially modern ones obliged to elaborate comprehensive electoral programs for democratic support, could easily succumb to the temptation to call "Catholic" whatever might appeal to the voters. On the other, she feared that broad partisan electoral programs would make being Catholic seem to demand support for all manner of public policies about which believers could legitimately disagree and which might therefore unnecessarily turn potential converts away from the misrepresented Faith.

Already by the turn of the century, the Holy See had come to the conclusion that a suitable lay activity that could justly be given the name "Catholic" would have to be more lobby-like in character; a "Catholic Action" composed of a variety of organizations. Each of these would be entrusted with specific tasks — such as the defense of education — whose doctrinally solid character could clearly be identified for the sake of a proper purification of their precise "spaces" of life. This unambiguous, lobby-like Catholic Action would then be kept to the straight and narrow path under a firm and properly spiritually focused clerical control.

La Civiltà Cattolica gave instructive contemporary flesh to the spirit of this Roman position, first of all with respect to the Italian situation.[2] Articles in the journal from the 1920s clearly spelled out the Holy See's suspicion of the Italian *Popolari* Party, led — once again, to Rome's intense dislike — by a priest, Don Luigi Sturzo (1871–1959), and aided by a former member of the Austrian Parliament and postwar Italian citizen, Alcide de Gasperi (1881–1954). The *Civiltà* argued that maintenance of a liberal-democratic political order rather than the attainment of any specific Catholic «thesis» seemed to be the chief goal of the *Popolari*. This, in Rome's eyes, made it guilty of placing greater hope for the purification of society in the structures of a particular form of government — and one which in Italy had historically proven generally to be very anti-Catholic — than in the purifying effects of the Faith. Sturzo, de Gasperi, and the *Popolari* were, in effect, accused of compounding this error by playing a double game, seeking to convince Catholics that they had an obligation to support the party program as believers, while simultaneously making a purely secular appeal for the backing of non-believing Italians. Moreover, the *Civiltà* did not appear to have had confidence in this non-Catholic "Catholic"

[2] See, J. Rao, "A Sketch".

party's ability to fend off what, once again, was indeed seen by the Holy See to be the greater evil: the radicalization of the Italian socialist movement, to the ultimate benefit of the communists.

Articles in the *Civiltà* concerning France and *l'Action Française* gave a second important insight into the Roman attitude regarding proper Catholic political activity in the interwar era, but they require a bit of background to understand. Anticlericalism had gained great influence over the Third Republic from the late 1870s onwards, reaching its peak with the unilateral denunciation of the Concordat of Napoleon in 1905 and its after effects. Anticlerical policies had aroused great bitterness against the existing government among the faithful, particularly over questions involving Catholic education and the religious congregations that had been active in providing it. Although the *Union Sacrée* during the war had eased these tensions a good deal, they nevertheless flared anew in the 1920s.

French believers never developed anything like the network of lay organizations to be found in Germany. Still, they had created certain groups that seemed to fit into the papal model of "Catholic Action". And many Catholics in the interwar period actively took part in the *La Ligue des Droits du religieux Ancien Combattant* and the *Fédération Nationale Catholique*, both of them focused primarily on fighting for Catholic schools and the religious orders needed to staff them.

Before the First World War Frenchmen had also been attracted to Marc Sangnier's (1873–1950)'s more broadly political *Sillon*, as well as the above-mentioned *Action Française* of Charles Maurras. The first of these movements had been created in 1894 in response to Leo XIII's call for a French Catholic hypothesis-like "rallying" to support of the Republic in order to work within it to purge it of its anticlerical tendencies. But it was condemned by St. Pius X in 1910 for falling prey to the repeatedly reproved error of treating a political system—in this case, the democratic system—as itself redemptive, and thereby more important than the Faith for the purification of society.

Maurras' *Action Française,* founded in 1899, gradually came to refer to a daily newspaper of that name, the school of thought it promoted, and a league for practical political and social action. Although the movement as a whole suffered from the vigorous papal rebuke of December of 1926, it was actually the newspaper and the school of thought that was the object of the pope's attack, as noted in the pages of *La Civiltà Cattolica*. Amidst a rather exaggerated assault on the movement's classicism, what the journal once again insisted was at stake was a placing of a political system—in this case, the monarchical—above the spiritual in importance: a *politique d'abord*, The basic error was said to be worsened by the fact that even though the non-Catholic leader of the movement admittedly gave the Catholic Church a major role in a legitimate French monarchy, he justified it on positivist grounds, merely as a force for social order and not as the teacher of the world. Catholics were thus—as in Italy, but in a different manner—made to feel obliged to support a movement built upon non-Catholic and even potentially anti-Catholic principles.

Rome's attitude, given clout by her abandonment of the *Popolari*, papal condemnation of major aspects of the work of the *Action Française*, and, even more so, by direct diplomatic negotiation between the Vatican and the governments of individual countries in Europe, aroused a great deal of resentment on the part of local Catholic lay activists. Despite the obvious complaint that the Holy See could not possibly understand all of the peculiar conditions affecting public life in every nation around the globe, questions regarding its interference in what ought to be a primarily lay-directed secular activity in a dangerously clericalist and therefore itself ultimately anti-Catholic manner also emerged.

One can easily grasp why this was the case. For, despite Rome's solid doctrinal teaching, her commitment to working for the victory of the Catholic "thesis" under the conditions of the interwar "hypothesis" does seem to have been open to suspicion. Theoretical speculations on how the thesis could be put into practice were certainly never a particular Vatican strong point. Even the Holy See's apparent interest in the importance of broad cultural issues does not appear to have translated into much practical labor. It is very difficult, to take but one example, to uncover anything impressive undertaken by the Papal Academy designed for precisely such a task.

Quite frankly, the interwar Papacy followed an "hypothesis" policy which had remained basically unchanged since the time of Leo XIII: that of finding some mere modus vivendi with all existing authorities, whoever they might be, generally for the sake of avoiding "greater evils". This was true even under St. Pius X, who approved of an agreement made with the liberal government of Italy to avoid the danger of a socialist victory in pre-First World War Italy; the so-called Gentiloni Pact. What counted was only some basic protection for the cult and its ministers to survive and for communism to be kept at bay. The result was the signing of thirteen Concordats and twenty-six Conventions and accords with varied forms of government—liberal, democratic, fascist, or authoritarian though they might be—the most important of which, at least for our purposes here, were the *Arreglos* with Mexico (1929), the Lateran Accords ending the Holy See's Risorgimento-born conflict with Italy (1929), and the *Reichskonkordat* with Germany in 1933. In fact, until brutally rebuffed in its efforts, Rome began the interwar period with a display of willingness to make a deal even with the communist government in Russia regarding the protection of the cult and its ministers.

Any kind of truly imaginative, energetic, militant effort to purify interwar Europe, especially one calling upon the aid of the laity to do so, would appear to have been shunned by the Vatican in favor of cooperation with existing powers, and this at a time when Rome was speaking very vigorously about the need to create a New

Christendom in missionary lands. Here, too, *La Civiltà Cattolica* is helpful in understanding the position of the Holy See. Articles in the journal praised the idea-less, obedience-focused character of fascism as offering an opportunity to guide the Duce down a proper direction on an issue-by-issue basis in a manner that avoided the possible ideological and political subversion of the Faith by outright Catholic movements.

In order for such an approach to be successful, Rome would actually have had to do something dramatic to insist upon the defense of the Catholic "thesis". And yet despite the many serious benefits granted, on paper, by the Lateran Accords, and the theoretical outrage of the Papacy at the ill treatment of Catholic Action in fascist Italy that almost immediately followed their implementation, the battles in the peninsula between Church and State amounted to temporary verbal clashes. There was precious little in the way of a Gramscian "counter-cultural" formation of the faithful useful to pressuring the "idea-less" leadership to bend to its will. What counted, once again, was simply the basic survival of cult and clergy. Yet even a defense of the basic cult conducted primarily by the laity was not greeted with enthusiasm. Here we have the example of the Mexican situation, where an American brokered agreement with the anti-Christian government was preferred to any fervent support of the Cristeros.

In sum, the papal policy in the interwar period simply did not work. It demonstrated a kind of faith in written documents more liberal than Catholic in character. Admittedly, negotiating with the powers-that-be was a clear necessity, if only for dealing with diocesan changes required by changing borders after the end of the world conflict. But government after government violated the agreements that had been painstakingly negotiated, that of Germany included. Pius XI swiftly became so vehemently anti-Nazi in consequence as to vary the policy described above, giving Engelbert Dollfuss' openly Catholic lay movement the kind of backing he generally did not wish to provide elsewhere, as a means of keeping the greater National Socialist menace out of Austria. But one wonders whether he regretted the fact that at the crucial moment of Hitler's establishment of his power in 1933, he opted for a Party of Order solution in Germany, regarding him as the only statesman in Europe who fully understood the evils of communism.

Perhaps worst of all, given its long-term effects, the Roman condemnation of the *Action Française*, only lifted in 1939 after the damage had long been done, did nothing to prevent the victory of the *politique d'abord* mentality. Aside from alienating many Catholics, who now saw the only hope for their particular political views to succeed as involving the same kind of reliance on the fascists that the *Civiltà* had baptized in the 1920s, what it also accomplished was a resurrection of the «democratic politics first» position of the *Sillon*. This then played an enormous role in the reshaping of a French episcopacy more and more open to a democratic secularist vision of society, along with their "higher education" in what this might actually mean by intellectual forces to be mentioned in more detail below; an episcopacy, which, through men like Achille Lienart (1884–1973), appointed Archbishop of Lille in 1928, was to be one of the central radicalizing forces of Second Vatican Council.

Rome, in short, opted for a general policy of fitting in with whatever Party of Order force worked best. In doing so, she was in a much better position to protect herself from policy criticism than ever before in history, due to the added strength that came from popular Catholic exaggeration of what was owed in the way of obedience to "infallible" papal governance since First Vatican Council, enhanced even further by the exaggerations of the anti-Modernist campaign. The Holy See's abandonment of any militant, specifically Catholic purification of the interwar order is especially ironic, given the fact that the revival movement of the nineteenth century, angered by the weak conformism of national episcopacies, had vigorously fostered the ultramontanist and infallibilist campaigns, seeing in Rome precisely the force that would guarantee support for commitment to full realization of the "thesis".

Not surprisingly, the interwar performance of local bishops as counter-cultural architects of a purified Catholic society was not a stellar one either. There was little to indicate any overwhelming movement away from their nineteenth century conformism. Fresh from an almost unanimous, enthusiastic support of the justice of their various opposing countries' war involvement, prelates generally continued to go with the national flow rather than courageously trying to call its unacceptable currents to task. I will have more to say about this below with respect to the situation in the United States. Suffice it to say at the moment that one of the most organized of national episcopacies in Europe, that of Germany, joined Rome in missing its opportunity at least to attempt to halt the National Socialist takeover when it might have been stopped, in the confusing months prior to January of 1933—primarily, once again, out of "Party of Order" considerations. Yes, there was some sign of episcopal energy later, in fighting the consequences of Nazi eugenics, but *Gleichshaltung* had by then rendered the formerly powerful German Catholic Church and her network of lay associations a shadow of their former self.

What can we say about the record of the network of movements and organizations whose existence began our discussion of the Catholic response to the interwar situation? We have already seen that these continued to have an impact in small countries like Portugal and Austria, committed to international cooperation and Catholic corporatist ideas, although whatever happened here, as we have now cited Salazar and Dollfuss as lamenting, was incapable of succeeding unless the Great Powers were on their side. And mention has also been made of yeoman efforts in defense of the cult, clergy, education, and social life in general in larger countries such as France, Mexico, and Spain.

In all fairness, however, I think it has to be admitted that the Papacy *was* correct in pinpointing many problems in lay Catholic political and social activity, especially concerning the flirtation with *politique d'abord*. Even if, for prudential "hypothesis" reasons, a *politique d'abord* policy might temporarily have been of benefit to the Catholic cause in one nation or another, the temptation to adopt it as a principle seemed often irresistible. The "Catholic" *Popolari were* indeed a problem in their adulation of liberal democracy, just as the spirit of the *Sillon* in France before the First World War and in its renewed influence after 1926 were dangerous in the extreme. The flip-flops of the Catholic Centre Party in Germany, giving substance to Bismarck's complaint about it representing every opinion imaginable depending upon what "worked", politically, for its various factions, was often painful to observe. Throughout its history, its deputies had offered support for everything from what was truly in line with the «thesis» to the backing of extreme nationalist, liberal capitalist, and Marxist outlooks, with the Party of Order principle in the interwar period always playing a central role.

Sadly, the presumption that the purification of life in a Catholic manner would somehow come from an uncritical dedication to the heroic cause of a Redeemer System, a Redeemer-King, a Redeemer-General, or even the redemptive "roar of the fascisti" was too common to make maintenance of a distance from potential allies a regular hallmark of the official movements of the era.[3] Yet, without that proper distance, the baptizing of non- or anti-Catholic recipes for purification as the Catholic thesis was a constant threat. And it was a threat that ultimately was dramatically realized, after the Second World War, with reference to the two fresh secularist competitors on the purification scene in 1918, America and Russia, in the form of a then "matured" Pluralism and Soviet Communism.

---

[3] See Rao, "A Sketch", section IV.

C. THE PARTICULAR PLURALIST THREAT

One ought to begin a discussion of Pluralism by noting that Europe already possessed a pluralist model before the First World War in The Netherlands. Nineteenth century battles of secularist forces versus a pro-religious Catholic-Protestant alliance had created what was referred to in that country as the "pillar system", which reflected many of the elements that were proclaimed as positive pluralist goals. Through this system, all Dutchmen were educated and, in effect, lived out their lives, in a Catholic, Protestant, or a secularist "pillar" of society, according to the principles approved by each of these. Pillarization seemed to work.

Nevertheless, its survival was dependent upon each of the pillars honestly leaving the others their independent space, and their avoidance of any internal subversion. The Catholic pillar would have required something more nourishing to feed on than the clerical-cult-devotional mentality prevalent in The Netherlands to understand how to defend itself from the determined aggression and subversion — particularly subversion — it eventually faced. Moreover, even if better prepared, it would, as Salazar could have pointed out to it, have had a hard time fending off the more destructive form of Pluralism coming from a great outside power: namely, the United States.

Although the *Civiltà* and her allies had critiqued "the American way" later referred to as Pluralism from the 1850s onwards, a very useful *native* guide to the character of its underlying poisons can be found in President Calvin Coolidge's address to the American Society of Newspaper Editors in Washington, D.C. on January 17, 1925.[4] Here, the president explains how the splendor of the United States as a land where the supreme cause of individual liberty had

---

[4] Calvin Coolidge: "Address to the American Society of Newspaper Editors, Washington, D.C.," January 17, 1925. Online by Gerhard Peters and John T. Woolley, The American Presidency Project. http://www.presidency.ucsb.edu/ws/?pid=24180.

triumphed over governmental tyranny provided the basic framework for the particular freedom enjoyed by the American press.

Now the Americans, Coolidge assures his audience, are an idealistic people. But their idealism never precludes a concern for "practical" affairs, with the press itself understanding that its very survival is tied up with a cultivation of "business". This is especially important in the United States because "the chief business of the American people is business. They are profoundly concerned with producing, buying, selling, investing and prospering in the world": in other words, with *"business d'abord"*.

Coolidge dismisses any fears regarding the dangers coming from a business mentality—which in the press's case might center on the threat of collusion with the wealthy, and complicity in dragging the public's attention down to profitable but ultimately rather debasing material concerns. For rather than cheapening existence, the entire business project enables men and women to realize the intense and ennobling American idealism that I have already noted Coolidge as identifying above:[5]

> It is rare indeed that the men who are accumulating wealth decay. It is only when they cease production, when accumulation stops, that an irreparable decay begins. Wealth is the product of industry, ambition, character and untiring effort. In all experience, the accumulation of wealth means the multiplication of schools, the increase of knowledge, the dissemination of intelligence, the encouragement of science, the broadening of outlook, the expansion of liberties, the widening of culture. Of course, the accumulation of wealth cannot be justified as the chief end of existence. But we are compelled to recognize it as a means to well nigh every desirable achievement. So long as wealth is made the means and not the end, we need not greatly fear it. And there never was

[5] Coolidge, in *Ibid*.

a time when wealth was so generally regarded as a means, or so little regarded as an end, as today.

Here, in a concise nutshell, the Chief Executive reproduces the mainstream Moderate Enlightenment, Whig, liberal, Anglo-American understanding of the relationship of the individual and society, with its insistence upon an intimate connection of free, practical, profitable activity and the high-minded consequences of nurturing it. This pleasant tale defines the good polis to be that which holds individual freedom to be its driving force, knows that that liberty will be used chiefly to gain wealth, but rests secure in the conviction that the wealth attained is the *sine qua non* for supporting unquestionable, traditional, higher goals: the intellectual and spiritual exaltation of the human person and the world in which he lives.

Personally, I do not doubt that President Coolidge is honest in his expectation that the philanthropic "dissemination of intelligence" and "encouragement of science" he lauds would support a number of higher, traditional goals *in his day*. These goals would have been defined by the "basic common sense" that the Whig, Anglo-American society of 1925 continued to treat as defending obvious "givens", and which did, indeed, still possess some influence over its citizens *at that time*.

Unfortunately, the substance of that remaining "obvious common sense", along with the higher and traditional goals so readily funded by a freely sought wealth, was constantly being whittled away at and dragged downwards by the materialist weightiness of the Whig concept of freedom. It was already much worn away in 1925 as compared with 1900, and Coolidge himself points to its basic intellectual and spiritual emptiness in his address to the editors. For in this talk he indicates that "the idealism of the American people is idealism"—providing no further defining guide to the idealism of individuals other than the telling fact that it is always "practical".

We have no time now fully to indicate what the effects of an unchecked American pluralist development would be on the cultural plane. Plato describes some of them brilliantly in *The Republic* in his discussion of "democratic man". Besides, we can observe them all around us every moment of every day in our own moment in time. Suffice it to say for now that it stimulates the creation of a pseudo-culture built upon an immense amount of indiscriminate kinds of self-humiliating, individual, elitist, or mass supported decadent elements, whether in the form of pornography, low level kitsch, or overbearing expressions of raw power, and in every realm of life, from music and film to architecture to social manners. Anything generating wealth is culturally good; anything not, a waste of time. Those wanting an internal American critique of the products and social manners this culture puts on display can look for a more detailed elaboration of the problem in Sinclair Lewis' (1885–1951) *Babbit* (1922) or in some of H.L. Mencken's (1880–1956) essays, such as *The Libido for the Ugly* and *On Being an American*.

The sole obstacle to the spiritual decay of a "practical idealism" in a Whig—and that means John Locke, and behind him an Enlightenment, Reformation, Nominalist, and Gnostic—driven society is the maintenance of the conventional agreement of the existing community. This can provide a powerful brake on any corrosive development due *either* to the continued strength of forces that do not necessarily grasp the full logical consequences of a polis with no substantive existence aside from the wishes of individual, liberty-obsessed, business-focused "idealists" and therefore continue to attack them according to long-established norms, *or* to those who *do* recognize them, dig in their heels, and refuse to accept them. In practical terms, both forms of resistance require the doctrinal firmness of the Roman Catholic Church and her commitment to the primacy of the spirit in all political and social realms to survive and have an impact.

As much as Catholics overwhelmingly took for granted the existing political system within the United States, and, when given the opportunity to do so, happily militated within the ranks of the existing parties, they certainly engaged in some distinct social activism. To take perhaps the most important example, Catholics, whether practicing or not, were active — and *critically* active — in the budding American labor movement. Criticism of the economic problems of the country was most effectively linked together with the mainline of Catholic thought on social justice by Fr. John Ryan (1869–1945), an academic and social activist. Ryan was central to producing the so-called "bishops program" on social justice in 1919, coming out of the National Catholic War Conference, which became at the conclusion of the conflict the National Catholic Welfare Conference.

Still, the original foundation of the NCWC illustrated the conformism of American Catholics, similar to that of their fellow believers in Europe, and this despite quite laudable papal attempts to convince believers to stay above the battle. If the American government supported the war, the war was right, and Catholics were told by their bishops and the NCWC not to criticize it. Even the "papal viceroys", like O'Connell, sometimes appear to have played a kind of double game of their own, serving as conduits for Roman initiatives in some matters so as to leave the American bishops free to follow their own peculiar national path on everything else.

In fact, with a few notable exceptions, the national conformism of the American episcopacy was such as to make the local bishops generally hostile to the "bishops'" program. It was too "socialist" for them, and thereby anti-American and, *ipso facto*, anti-Catholic in character. They were ecclesiastical businessmen who had businessmen's goals for construction of churches and schools and sought approval for their "*business d'abord*" successes from the Establishment. Ryan was a danger to them. What they preferred was an integration into contemporary society, all too much in line with the flip side of the interwar isolationist mentality: the insistence upon the need for existing foreign elements to avoid being "divisive" and "integrate themselves" as good Americans. Catholics had the freedom to pursue their basic cult and their devotions under the guidance of a secular clergy. What more did they need from "the last, best hope of mankind"? "Americanism, liberal capitalism, the general moral consensus, and Sunday Mass, now and forever, one and inseparable" could easily have been inscribed on most bishops' banners.

Promotion of Catholic social justice in the United States seemed to get a new lease on life with the Great Depression and its effects both in Rome and at home. *Quadragesimo anno* (1931) gave new and better support to Catholic Social Doctrine positions than *Rerum novarum* (1891), which it commemorated, had ever done. Ryan and other Catholics, such as Fr. Charles Coughlin (1891–1979), a man who knew how to utilize the radio to spread a popular message, along with a few significant bishops, took heart with the victory of Franklin Delano Roosevelt and the institution of the New Deal. The National Recovery Administration, calling for a communal "war" effort, under General Hugh Johnson, with participants in its mission forming a so-called "Blue Army" symbolized by the display of a "Blue Eagle", whatever the motives of its creators might have been, reflected some clearly fascist elements, but in an American context that appeared to be quite open to the Catholic vision.

Ryan was destined to stand by Roosevelt throughout his time in office. Nevertheless, the condemnation of the first New Deal by the Supreme Court and its reorganization in a way that Fr. Coughlin deemed suitable to manipulation both by *international* capitalism and communism, brought the radio priest into a vocal opposition, not surprisingly condemned by conformist bishops urged on by the Administration. Dorothy Day (1897–1980) and Peter Maurin (1877–1949), whose newspaper, *The Catholic Worker*, was, for a time, the chief competitor of the communist *Daily Worker* in the

United States, were also concerned about a deeper change in the existing system in a way that emarginated them both ecclesiastically and politically.

A dedication to the cult, its devotional practices, and the protection of the clergy could do little to win America for Christ the King in the midst of the reigning non-divisive, integrating, conformist mentality. The best that could be accomplished, and this because the general moral consensus was still basically united in such a regard, was to tame gross immorality in the cinema through the Legion of Decency and the Code forced upon the Hollywood moguls. And this, as the United States moved into the Second World War, did not prevent American openness to all religious belief being praised with Catholic blessing, in films such as those about the modernist-minded Fr. Duffy in *The Fighting Sixty Ninth*, or the model cleric being depicted as the easy-going Bing Crosby in *Going My Way*. American Catholics, "integrated" into their society more than ever before in a period of real isolation from continued European influences, believed in the message of the "last, best hope of mankind" by 1945. They were ready to accept its complete equation with all the goals of the Faith, especially in the face of danger coming from "a greater evil": Soviet Communism.

D. THE "OUTER AND INNER MISSIONS" AND THE PECULIAR TEMPTATION OF MILIEU D'ABORD

We have seen why Catholic thinkers saw Marxist movements and their call for a purification of capitalist bourgeois decadence as more than understandable reactions to real injustice. On the other hand, *La Civiltà Cattolica* could not help but recognize in Soviet Communism, the second «new kid on the block» in 1918, a development of the same naturalist illness as all of the other Gnostic-Nominalist-Reformation-Enlightenment engendered competitors of the Catholic Church, that produced in America included. Here, instead of willful, individual capitalist exploiters of the people, it was the ideologues, operating through commissars and petty bureaucrats to manipulate the masses they claimed to serve, who were the active agents of irrational willfulness and purely materialist self-interest. Communism's cultural influence in the interwar period was enormous. This ran the gauntlet from the exaltation of overbearingly materialist raw power to that of a culturally permissive environment meant to reflect Marxist-Leninist progress and freedom: at least until the vision of Stalin and the demands of the First Five Year Plan inside the Soviet Union rendered the latter dangerous to dictatorship and production. It differed from the raw power adulation of the American skyscraper and relentless American cultural permissiveness only in that the New World expression was promoted, praised, or at least accepted in so far as it created personal wealth. It is interesting to note, in passing, that the cultural pressure to demonstrate one's undying "happiness" at being "part of the gang" was a common element in the Soviet, American, and fascist atmosphere. In any case, anyone being shaped culturally by conformism to such forces was not being shaped in a way that gave glory to Christ as King.

Despite the solid doctrinal rejection of Marxism-Leninism and the general Catholic practical cooperation with representatives of the two versions of the Party of Order noted above, there were certain anti-liberal, anti-fascist believers ready to join the communist call for a Popular Front against the advances of Mussolini, Hitler, and their imitators in the interwar period. Moreover, the period 1918–1939 was rich in intellectual forces constructing an argument that could easily lend support to such a choice. This argument presented a new approach towards "Catholic" purification based upon a spirit that might be labeled *milieu d'abord*: "milieu first". And it was through the progress of that spirit, and the enchantment with the milieux and mystiques of the victors of the Second World War that a perverse equation of Catholic purification with that offered not just by Soviet Communism but also by the American Pluralism was to come about. This would bring the revival movement of the nineteenth century to a tragic and resounding end and lull Catholics back into their eighteenth century dogmatic slumber. Ironically, however, discussing this perversion requires a brief return to the revival movement in question to elaborate.

Nineteenth century Catholic activists had recruited into their ranks men of the deepest and most unquestionable zeal for militant evangelization and transforming action both abroad and at home. They wanted success and saw this as urgently needed to prevent man as opposed to Christ becoming king of the world. Nineteenth century Catholics—following the example of militant Protestants—began to speak of the overall enterprise of evangelization as being directed down two distinct paths: that of the Outer Missions (focused on bringing the Faith to non-Christian peoples) and the Inner Missions (those aimed at the secularized populations of what were considered generally as already Christianized lands). The *milieu d'abord* vision grew out of speculations regarding how best to succeed in both of these fields of endeavor.[6]

Outer missionaries had always operated under a variety of irritations coming from both internal Church disputes regarding jurisdiction and episcopal authority, as well as from European colonial powers aiding or limiting evangelization based upon reasons of State. Certain groups, like the Moslems and the bulk of the Chinese population, seemed invulnerable to conversion. Building upon the experience of generations of missionaries in the tradition of Matteo Ricci, a number of those engaged in the Outer Missions became more and more convinced of the need for a deeper effort to "get under the skins" of the groups whom they were trying to evangelize—to "inculturate" the Faith, as one would say in our own day. They hoped that in doing so, Christianity could be stripped of any appearance as an alien force, and be viewed as best suited

---

[6] The rest of the argument in this article comes from J. Rao, *The Black Legends*, pp. 563–630. Only direct citations are specially footnoted.

to the natural development and perfection of the communities in question instead.

The names Charles de Foucauld (1858–1916) and Vincent Lebbe (1877–1940) are very important to Catholic developments in this area with respect to evangelization of the Moslems and the Chinese, and one might also add to theirs that of Mgr. John Österreicher (1904–1993), whose *Pauluswerk* focused upon conversion of the Jews in interwar Europe. Catholic clerics in Münster, Louvain, Lille, and Paris played a major role in this enterprise as well, imitating Protestant evangelists in the creation of "missiology": the deeper study of all of the elements needed to understand the peoples whose conversion was being pursued, including ethnology, sociology, psychology, and anthropology.

We have seen that missiology was added to the curriculum of the Gregorian in 1932, and the Holy See encouraged many other new initiatives in the missionary field. It was stimulated to do so by the conviction that Europe was committing suicide, thus requiring serious work for preparing the foundation of a "New Christendom" outside its borders. Benedict XV, in *Quo efficacius* (1920) and *Maximum illud* (1922), and Pius XI in *Romanorum pontificum* (1922) both stressed the need for all Christians — not just the clergy — to recognize their responsibility to build this New Christendom as "outer missionaries". Peter Canisius' canonization and the memory of his never-ending travels inside Europe were offered as an indication of the self-sacrificing activity demanded of such a labor in foreign fields.

Rome's deeper commitment to the task led it to call the Society for the Propagation of the Faith, along with experts in missiology, to establish their headquarters in the Eternal City. An international congress of missiology was held there in 1922, the two hundredth anniversary of the foundation of the Congregation for the Propagation of the Faith. Support for the concept of inculturation was demonstrated not just by means of the strengthening of the higher education of indigenous clergy at the *Urbaniana*, but also by the consecration of the first Chinese bishops in 1926 and the lifting of the prohibition against practicing the so-called Chinese rites in 1935, and those prevalent in Japan in the following year.

A new kind of Catholic focus on the Inner Missions, once again also aided by imitation of Protestant efforts in this regard, developed out of work that began in Italy and Belgium from the 1890s onwards. The *Opera dei Congressi*, the nationwide Catholic lay movement dealing with the problems presented by the new, anticlerical Kingdom of Italy, gave birth in 1896 to an organization concerned directly with the youthful *milieu*, the *Federazione Universitaria Cattolica Italiana* or FUCI. Somewhat later, the Belgian priest, Fr. Joseph Cardijn (1886–1967), became convinced of the need to create a "specialized Catholic Action" that distinguished milieu from milieu and developed a fervor within each of these specific ambiences giving birth to evangelists ready to bring the light of Christ to others like them in the world at large. His *Jeunesse Ouvrières Chrétienne* (1924), aimed uniquely at young workers, was very influential as a model in the "years between". Fr. Jaques Sevin (1882–1951), along with a fellow French Jesuit, Fr. Paul Donceour (1880–1961), following the model for guiding youth offered by Baden-Powel in Britain several decades earlier, were crucial to the foundation and guidance of the very important Catholic Scouting Movement in France in 1920.

Laborers in the Outer Missions were worried about the effects on their work in environments made still more difficult due to the influence of growing native religious revivals, along with disgruntlement over the mass conscription and stricter control of populations disturbing life in the colonial world in the First World War. Inner Missionaries grew more militant after 1918 due to the fact that their lack of success was made painfully obvious by the general indifference to religion that activists—who had really not ventured forth from their own limited milieux beforehand—encountered among their fellow soldiers in the trenches during the conflict. Everything from the libertinism of frontline soldiers to their enthusiasm regarding the news from Russia made the meager Catholic efforts to change men's minds and hearts appear pathetic in comparison. Lay activists sympathized with the outrage of clerics and seminarians compelled by a number of belligerent countries to fight during the war and forced by the Church to undergo a purification rite for having done so afterwards, believing that this all too clearly revealed a failure on the part of the ecclesiastical authorities to understand the realities imposed by the outside world upon contemporary Catholics.

A third force that contributed to the creation of the *milieu d'abord* approach in a manner that tied in with the concerns of the Outer and Inner Missionaries was the Liturgical Movement. Very much associated with the nineteenth century revival of interest in the Roman Rite and Gregorian Chant—as with the work of Dom Gueranger at Solesmes in France—this had expanded to involve a popular education of the laity ensuring its deeper participation in the Mass that had been blessed by Pope St. Pius X. A popularly understood liturgy became still more important in the minds of liturgists seeing it as a major ritual tool in the quest for purification reaching fever pitch during the First World War. This, in turn, then stimulated discussions regarding how the liturgy, by means of an emphasis on the Roman Rite's "noble simplicity", could be made more accessible to the average person, and, through deeper appreciation of the specific needs of distinct groups, to the different milieux of missionary lands and Specialized Catholic Action. Dom Lambert Beauduin (1873–1960) in Belgium; Abbot Ildefons Hergewegen (1874–1946) of Maria Laach, Romano Guardini (1885–1968), and Josef Jungmann (1889–1975) in Germany; and Maurice de la Taille (1872–1933), Jean Maydieu, (1900–1955), Victor Dillard (1897–1945), and Paul Donceur in France were all active in this project.

Finally, ecumenical initiatives on the part of liturgists and certain Catholic prelates and intellectuals eager to understand the causes of continued Christian division also aided the *milieu d'abord* mentality. Beauduin, who created an ecumenical minded journal called *Irénikon* in 1926, took part in the Malines Conversations of 1921–1927 with Anglican High Churchmen. Numerous French clerics and laity were eager to engage in dialogue with the Russian Orthodox exiles active at the Institut de Saint-Serge in Paris, a discussion entertained by Anglicans and Orthodox in Britain, both clerical and lay, through formation of the Fellowship of St. Alban and St. Sergius. The Russian Orthodox, in particular, through the nineteenth century concept of *sobornost*, encouraged a Christian mentality that was community minded in a way that evoked aspects of the *milieu d'abord* position.

The interwar years offered an influential explanation for how to correct the lack of success experienced by the Outer and Inner missionaries, with crucial consequences for the Liturgical and Ecumenical Movements as well, through the arguments of representatives of the personalist movement. Personalism, as it developed at the time, perhaps ought to be referred to as a tendency rather than a specific idea. Many diverse circles of thinkers used the term, and some of the themes associated with it. It is in this sense that Jacques Maritain (1882–1973), principally thought of in conjunction with Thomism and Integral Humanism, may also be cited as a personalist.

More directly associated with the movement were men such as Emmanuel Mounier (1905–1950), editor of the journal *l'Esprit*, whose so-called Communitarian Personalism, like Maritain's somewhat related Integral Humanism, was destined to have a wide impact beyond Europe in radicalizing the Catholic camp after the Second World War. Mounier had pre-war contacts with a kaleidoscope of thinkers engaged in similar speculations: Jean Danielou (1905–1974), the future cardinal; Jean Guitton (1901–1999), who would one day become a close friend and advisor to Pope Paul VI; Nicholas Berdyaev (1874–1948) — the most important representative of the mystical, anti-scholastic, anti-legalist, Russian Orthodox position — and a network of friends who met at Jacques Maritain's home outside Paris; Henri Daniel-Rops (1901–1965) and his fellow members of the organization *Ordre Nouveau* (New Order); Belgians inspired by the "spiritualized Socialism" of Henri de Man (1885–1953); proponents of European cooperation like Otto Abets (1903–1958), the future Nazi ambassador to a defeated France; and a group of "revolutionary National Socialists" gathered in the early 1930s around the Hitler rivals Gregor (1892–1934) and Otto Strasser (1897–1974).

Interwar Personalism had its roots in late eighteenth, nineteenth, and early twentieth century romantic and vitalist thought concerning the importance of "energy" and "action" as guides to truth. Lamennais' heritage played a major role in transmitting such interest among Catholics, and modernist thinkers in further disseminating it. The emphasis upon energy and action as a program for life was, once again, enhanced still more by meditation upon the experience of those front-line soldiers during the First World War who heroically sacrificed themselves together in a common cause despite their divisions into so many different religious, political, and social factions at home.

Insofar as one can summarize a highly variegated vision, communitarian personalism can be said to argue that the individual, trapped inside his private intellectual and behavioral concerns, is a dead man. To become a full "person", capable of realizing his deepest potential and fulfilling his true destiny, he must find a way to get out of himself and his deadening introspective existence. This he can achieve by diving into the richer life provided by communities — milieux — and the "natural values" they incarnate and pursue. Which communities? Which natural values? The communities and natural values in question were those that moved men to cohesive, energetic, effective action by means of a unique, discernable, vital, milieu "mystique". Action in union with such mystiques transformed limited, sterile individuals into truly microcosmic personalities.

Catholic personalists with such ideas saw the kind of believer who approached his faith as a set of precepts that might be studied intellectually and then put into practice on the individual level as a self-crippling, introspective personality. Nineteenth and early twentieth century "revival" Catholicism, with its emphasis on speculative theology, private devotions, and concern for individual sanctification, was said to produce just this type of faithful. A better grasp of the Christian Faith, a richer life, and a full perfection of "personhood" required something quite different. It demanded the individual's abandonment to the "mystiques" of the energetic and highly effective milieux-communities that he saw around him. Yes, these might appear to be promoting *purely* "natural values". Nevertheless, the energies that they unleashed, and the successes they enjoyed, demonstrated that there was something more at work through them: the providential power of the Holy Spirit in history. The Catholic missionary's task was that of "witnessing" to his faith in a quiet, humble fashion, by nurturing the natural value of the community to which he was sent so that it might be brought to its innate perfection. Such witness would also be enriching for him, since he would learn things about Christ and the movement of the Holy Spirit in history that he could never have known before plunging into the mystique and life of the vital group in question.

One day, the Holy Spirit would guarantee the "convergence" of all these seemingly contradictory milieux and their mystiques. The result would be the establishment of a community of communities capable of producing what would, in effect, be super-persons, the grandest transformation to which humanity has ever submitted. The seeming nightmare provided by a variety of often quite violent twentieth century forces hostile to the Faith was actually a splendid call to hope. One was witnessing through their maturation the bloody birth of a true collective being of men; mysterious indeed, but Spirit-guided and therefore eminently Catholic.

Believers must not sit in judgment of milieux-mystiques on the path to convergence. For they could not even fully know what the Catholic Faith entailed and where the Holy Spirit was leading it until the natural values that the various mystiques enshrined had all unfolded and then merged together. Rather than criticism, *total immersion* in energetic milieu, their communities and their mystiques was required. Such immersion demanded a root and branch obliteration of all previous education and practice that gave the militant missionary a different perspective from someone who was already a part of the providential community to which he was sent to witness. Reliance on the dry, intellectual, introspective teachings and private devotions of official Catholicism presented an obstacle to victory. Christ and His Spirit were to be found in the vital community and its mystique — not in textbooks of theology mulled over by self-limiting individuals who stubbornly refused to become truly active and effective persons.

Nineteenth-century Catholics opposed to Lamennais knew what to expect from *his* vision. Their critique, enunciated in the writings of the Jesuit editors of *La Civiltà Cattolica* and their allies, also points to the problems of Catholic personalism. All calls for submission to vital, active, milieu community's guidance from the time of Lamennais to that of Mounier have always entailed two consequences: first of all, the destruction of any means of distinguishing between a good and bad manifestation of communal energy; and, secondly, the determination, in practice, of what is or is not acceptable as a "natural value on the path to maturation" through the *Diktat* of charismatic interpreters of the "right kind of vitality". Tossing away the crutches of the self-crippling, introspective individual has regularly ended in immersion in anti-Christian community passions to begin with, and enslavement to the obsessions of "vanguards of the people" that arrogate to themselves the right to explain what a society "really" energetically feels forever thereafter.

"Spiritualization" of everything natural, as practiced by the interwar personalists, must end in the naturalization of a world that is really meant to undergo correction and purification in Christ. The progress of the Holy Spirit in history becomes merely another way of describing the triumph of the strongest human will. Morever, those accepting this approach are also helpless in combating the frightful willfulness of successful, charismatic, and criminal nineteenth and twentieth century ideologies—liberalism, communism, fascism, and American pluralism. In fact, those subscribing to this vision find themselves incapable of responding to any energetic fraud; "barren in the face of a Ramakrishna", as the much more cautious, Thomist, friend of philosophy, Jacques Maritain, complained.[7]

---

[7] J. Hellman, *Emmanuel Mounier and the New Catholic Left* (McGill-Queens, 1997), p. 42.

CHAPTER 5

The Interwar Spirit on the March to the Present: "Catholic" Purification as the Triumph of the Strongest, Mindless Will

A. THE WAR EXPERIENCE, PERSONALISM, AND THE NEW THEOLOGY

MANY PERSONALISTS GREETED THE early fascist victories of the Second World War hopefully. A number of them, long convinced of the innate weaknesses of the liberal bourgeois "established disorder," expressed little surprise over the conquests of Nazi Germany. What really concerned them was whether Catholicism could find some way to turn a potentially apocalyptic "purification" down the proper pathway. For fascism was seen to be a "monstrous prefiguration" of the new personalist humanity waiting to be born. It clearly revealed the presence of strong will, virile manliness, self-sacrifice to the community, and even, in the context of the war effort, a commitment to the construction of that European-wide super society which many thought to be crucial to a better New World Order.

Pétain's so-called National Revolution was appreciated by many French personalists both because of its anti-liberal bourgeois character and its freedom from the more gross "materialist" aspects of Nazism. They hoped to make Vichy France a wartime laboratory for educational and evangelical schemes designed to reshape the world in a spiritual way. One major example of educational experimentation incorporating both contemporary Catholic ideas as well as features of the fascist *Ordensburgen* — the castle training centers for the new elite of German youth — was the *École Nationale des Cadres* at the Château Bayard above the village of Uriage, near Grenôble. Founded in the waning months of 1940, this institution became especially significant by June of 1941, when the Vichy regime determined to require a session at the *École* for all future high government functionaries.

The teachings of a vast array of Catholic luminaries and their fellow travelers were marshaled under the banner of the National Revolution to play a role at Uriage. Still, under the day-to-day direction of Pierre Dunoyer de Segonzac (1906–1968) and the guidance of the Study Bureau of Hubert Beuve-Mery (1902–1989), Mounier's "communitarian personalism" was central therein. This was true even after political problems led to Mounier's removal from its staff. For his vision continued to prosper through the similar teaching of his friend, Jean Lacroix (1900–1986), and their common master, Jacques Chevalier (1882–1962), professor at Grenôble and sometime Vichy Minister of Education.

Allied with personalism at Uriage was the radicalizing influence of the budding New Theology. This arrived via the Dominican houses of Saulchoir and Latour-Maubourg, the Jesuit center at Fourvières, the journals *La vie intellectuelle*, *Sept* and *Temps present*, the French scouting movement, and specialized Catholic Action groups stimulated through the activity of Joseph Cardijn with young Christian workers in Belgium. Segonzac and Beuve-Mery had frequented such circles before the war. They happily brought to Uriage priests like Henri de Lubac (1896–1991), Jean Maydieu (1900–1955), Victor Dillard (1897–1945), and Paul Donceour (1880–1961). These men, in turn, introduced students to the writings of Lamennais, Henri Bergson (1859–1941), Maurice Blondel

(1861–1949), Charles Péguy (1873–1914), Marie-Domenique Chenu (1895–1990), Yves Congar (1904–1995), Karl Adam (1876–1966), Romano Guardini (1885–1968), Charles de Foucauld and, perhaps more importantly than anyone else, Pierre Teilhard de Chardin (1881–1955). Uriage also had links, direct and indirect, with Frs. Louis Joseph Lebret (1897–1966) and Jacques Loew (1908–1999), founders of the Catholic social movement, *Economie et Humanisme*, which was destined for a significant "progressive" future in Latin America as well as in Europe.

Students at the *École* were thus familiarized with currents of biblical, historical, spiritual, liturgical and philosophical thought that, while marginal at the moment, would become immensely powerful and instrumental in guiding the Second Vatican Council and the post-conciliar Church. And this team, "ensconced in a chateau up in the mountains with a commission to completely rethink and transform the way France educated its young people", was absolutely and enthusiastically convinced that it was *the* prophetic guide to the future.[1]

Correction and transformation of the world, according to the doctrine taught at Uriage, was, once again, dependent upon the creation of "persons" as opposed to "individuals." Hence Uriage's stunning ecumenism, testified to in a myriad of ways. One could see Segonzac's ability "to form friendly relations, on the spiritual plane, with Protestants, Catholics, Jews, Moslems, agnostics," since he "preferred (rooted) people ... in their own setting, in their own culture".[2] Uriage's Charter proclaimed the truth that "believers and non-believers are, in France, sufficiently impregnated with Christianity", so that "the better among them could meet, beyond revelations and dogmas, at the level of the community of persons,

---

[1] Hellman, *The Knight Monks, of Vichy France: Uriage, 1940–1945* (McGill-Queens, 1997) p. 56.

[2] Ibid., p. 83

in the same quest for truth, justice and love".³ And Mounier, in full-fledged Teilhardian rapture, prophesied the mysterious and convoluted growth of the "perfect personal community," where "love alone would be the bond" and "no constraint, no vital or economic interest, no extrinsic institution" would play a role:⁴

> Surely [development] is slow and long when only average men are working at it. But then heroes, geniuses, a saint come along: a Saint Paul, a Joan of Arc, a Catherine of Siena, a Saint Bernard, or a Lenin, a Hitler and a Mussolini, or a Gandhi, and suddenly everything picks up speed…[H]uman irrationality, the human will, or simply, for the Christian, the Holy Spirit suddenly provides elements which men lacking imagination would never have foreseen.
>
> May the democrat, may the communist, may the fascist push the positive aspirations which inspire their enthusiasm to the limit and plenitude.

As John Hellman explains, "Mounier's belief that there was an element of truth in all strong beliefs coincided with Teilhard's vision of the inevitable spiritualization of humanity".⁵ This belief, Uriage as a whole made its own.

Let it be emphasized once more that the message taught at Uriage was not a rational one. Its ultimate justification was the prophetic intuition of teachers giving witness to the coming New Order and their strength of will in leading men to creative action. Any appeal to logic, either in support or criticism of strongly willed commitment to the natural values they approved was dismissed as either belaboring the given or as dangerous, decadent, crippling, individualist scholastic pedantry. Better to bury the temptations of

---

3 Hellman, *The Knight Monks*, p. 59.
4 Hellman, *Mounier*, pp. 85, 90.
5 Ibid., p. 128.

a sickly rationalism through the development of the obvious virtue of "manliness" — a virtue defined in completely anti-intellectual ways: the ability to leap onto a moving streetcar; to ride a bicycle up the steep hill to the *École* like Jacques Chevalier; to look others "straight in the eye" and "shake hands firmly"; to endure the sweat-filled regimen labeled *décrassage* devised for students under the inspiration of General Georges Hébert; to sing enthusiastically around the evening fire in the Great Hall; to know how to "take a woman"; and, always, to feel pride in "work well done." Such manliness was said to have deep spiritual meaning in and of itself, aspects of which were elaborated in lectures like de Lubac's *Ordre viril, ordre chrétien* (*Virile Order, Christian Order*), and Chenu's book, *Pour être heureux, travaillons ensemble (For Happiness, Let Us Work Together).*[6]

Finally, let us stress that Uriage's teaching was unabashedly elitist. In fact, the particular mystique of the *École* was that of developing the natural value of leadership. "The select youth of Uriage" were said to be "the first cell of a new world introduced into a worn-out one"[7], "entrusted with the mission of bringing together the elite from all of the groups that ought to participate in the common task of reconstruction in the same spirit of collaboration".[8] Since they were destined to reveal the eternal supernatural significance of the natural values witnessed to by the mystique of all virile communities, Uriage students were in some sense priestly figures as well. Each class was consecrated and given a great man's name as talisman. Segonzac especially "took upon himself a certain sacerdotal role, even regarding the wives and children of his instructors".[9] This entailed also a "separation between the leaders, the lesser leaders, the lesser-lesser leaders, the almost leaders and the not-at-all leaders"

[6] Hellman, *The Knight Monks*, pp. 4–52, 68–92, 139–162.
[7] Ibid., p. 65.
[8] Ibid., p. 83.
[9] Ibid., p. 90.

irritating to some of the interns. "The central team," as one of them indicated, "were gods".[10]

Nevertheless, for those manly spirits ready to leap off of streetcars moving towards indeterminate destinations, sit down in a café, and indulge in a little logical scholastic debate, the education imparted at Uriage might easily seem to be *sacrificing* the corrective and transforming mission of Catholicism at the altar of fascism rather than taming the "monstrous prefiguration of the future" that it represented. But, then again, the student of Church History is all too familiar with such spiritually disguised labors on behalf of the Coalition of the Status Quo. He knows that this particular manifestation of an age-old phenomenon emerged out of the same concern to restore a shattered western social order by appeal to the non-rational will of virile communities stirred to action by charismatic prophets central to the school of Lamennais. And it was, of course, to this heritage that the teachers of Uriage appealed.

Yes, many of the particular obsessions of contemporary fascists may have been of secondary importance to the Catholic personalists we have been discussing, but the canonization of a submission of the individual to the will of the leaders of a non-rational community was common to both. What difference did it make if Uriage teachers employed Catholic-friendly words and phrases like "person" and the "Mystical Body of Christ" in their enterprise? How could one know what, exactly, these words and phrases signified when rigorous philosophical-theological examination of their meaning was ridiculed as decadent and unnecessary to men with "deep faith" working to lead men to the better world in the making? Alas, the consequences of this fascist mentality for Catholicism were, ironically, only fully to be seen when fascism itself was thought to have been unconditionally defeated, after 1945. And the postwar age that followed was to prove to be a time when the "business as

[10] Hellman, *The Knight Monks*, p. 75.

usual demands" of "nature as is" were to triumph more completely than at any moment since the conversion of the Roman Empire; an era when the very Mystical Body of Christ herself, the "salt of the earth", seemed to lose her savor — to the detriment both of true community and the dignity of the individual human person.

B. THE VICTORY OF THE MARXIST AND PLURALIST MYSTIQUES OVER THE CATHOLIC THESIS

Fascist Europe was doomed by the time that the Soviet Union and the United States were linked with Britain in the war against Germany. These first two countries were to prove to be the real victors in that conflict. Both found that that victory was useful as a postwar propaganda tool in demonizing the opponents of their guiding ideologies: Marxism-Leninism and Americanism — re-baptized in the postwar world under the more suitably international, freedom and diversity friendly name of "pluralism". All they needed to do in order to maintain this demonization was to keep the drama of the Second World War alive as a never-ending "current event". Memory of the war was to prove to be a "Punic terror" that might always be evoked to stimulate a fear sufficient to maintain unity among any of their wavering troops.

By repeatedly recalling the evils perpetrated by Hitler, the victorious ideologies were able to drive home the argument that everything non-Marxist or non-pluralist was, *ipso facto*, National Socialist; that anyone who opposed tyranny, bloodshed, and genocide had better fall in behind their banners and dread the consequences of breaking rank. Human awe in the face of victorious armed strength, combined with terror at the prospect of being labeled a fascist, badly crippled and even totally silenced opposition of any kind. The only weak point in this powerful ideological weaponry was the fact that it could be — and swiftly was — used by the two victors against one another as well as against their common enemies. Marxist-Leninists were the new fascists for the pluralists, and pluralists for the Marxist-Leninists—another example of the age-old divisions within a Grand Coalition of the Status Quo solidly unified only in its joint disdain for the corrective and purifying mission of the Word Incarnate.

Although Marxism-Leninism, for a time, seemed to match American pluralism in its appeal as victor, it was ultimately the latter force that won the contest for exploiting a good story about the good war on its behalf. Using the innate and often unconscious power and prestige that came from conquest, the United States worked mightily to reshape the spiritual, intellectual, economic, and social systems of Western Europe in order to channel them to the service of its own pluralist vision. What could be more appealing to a world worn out by the incalculable human suffering accompanying ideological hatred and deadly political conflict than the pluralist offer of a practical, pragmatic "method" for dealing with the diversity and divisions of modern life; a method guaranteeing freedom for all beliefs and cultures to co-exist peacefully, subject only to the dictates of a "basic common sense" ensuring "public order"? What could be more suitable than the peaceful, "free marketplace of ideas and life styles" that it cherished? Persecution would end and every tear would be wiped away. If attempts to resist such a magnificent vista were not indicative of sympathy for the genocidal madness of the defeated fascists, then they could only represent a state of insanity pure and simple.

Gradually, the influence of the pluralist message over every aspect of life, over every judgment regarding what one should think and how one should behave, became more and more inescapable. It was reinforced in daily imagery, from morning until night, from infancy until old age. So pervasive was it that the average youth in the Old World came to understand his counterpart in America even without a common spoken language and even as his own particular tradition became more and more incomprehensible to him. The pressure exerted upon individuals and institutions by the subtle and overt presuppositions and demands of the daily environment created by the American pluralist vision was, in short, overwhelming, rendering the idea of any protection against its ravages or any open resistance to it from any quarter whatsoever utterly utopian. This was a Defender of the Peace of whom the nominalists and regalists of the Late Middle Ages and the Reformation might truly be proud.

Many European Catholics were as awed and acquiescent before the victors as everyone else on the Old Continent. The enormous difficulties of explaining a Christian position built upon theological, philosophical, and cultural arguments rejected by them frustrated a second group of Catholics into silence. A third Catholic element did speak out against whichever of the two victorious ideologies it deemed more dangerous, while remaining quiet regarding the errors of the other, and eventually even praising its own similar acceptance of the demands of "nature as is". Yet another segment of the Catholic population, ashamed by the fact that some fellow believers had either been attracted by fascism or had seen in it a useful tool against a much more dangerous Marxist threat, enthusiastically embraced the message of the victors to compensate for sins which, uncontested, might be used as a pretext for casting aspersions upon the whole Church's honor. And, finally, the atmosphere created by the "good story" about the "good war" allowed misled Catholics who were actively committed to Marxism or pluralism an audience and an impact that they otherwise might never have had. This was especially true if those activists had performed courageous deeds during the great conflict that might give them enormous prestige in the postwar anti-fascist world.

Mention of this last group brings us back to the Catholic personalists. There is no denying that fascism, with its vibrancy, was intensely appealing to many personalists. But the dominant National Socialist strain of fascism was unavoidably and unacceptably tied to the *Volksgemeischaft*, and personalists, despite their other temptations, never succumbed to that of modern racism. After all, different races could be just as energetic in the support of their beliefs and traditions as the Nazis were of Aryan supremacy. In fact, it was precisely this truth that had led important missionaries into the personalist camp in the first place. In any case, a number of personalists courageously and openly opposed Nazi racism from the outset, both through membership in the Resistance Movement as well as in journals like the French *Témoignage chrétien*. They thereby gained understandable prestige as heroic exemplars for future generations.

Even more significant in assuring personalist condemnation of *all* of fascism, non-racist as well as racist, was the simple fact that it had not been sufficiently vital to win the Second World War. Through defeat it lost the credibility it had once possessed as an engine of success. Victory in that conflict had been carried off by the Soviet Union and the United States. One might thus legitimately conclude that Marxist-Leninist and American-guided communities were those that possessed the greatest vigor and successful energy — and therefore the infallible stamp of approval of the Holy Spirit.

Both conviction and prudence thus told personalists who had openly tried to collaborate with a non-racist fascism that the entire movement, at least as presently constituted, had to be jettisoned. Nowhere was this more felt than at Uriage. The deportation of French youth to forced labor camps, the increasing control by Germany of internal Vichy affairs, and the outright takeover of the Unoccupied Zone in the latter part of 1942 had already moved the leadership of the *École* closer to the growing Resistance Movement, long before allied victory was absolutely assured. This tendency matured by December of that year, when Uriage's enemies at Vichy managed to have it expelled from the Château Bayard.

But Uriage never did anything haphazardly. Building upon its sense of constituting a modern band of crusading knights, the exiled *École* leadership in 1943 created a Chivalric Order whose inner circle was bound by special vows of a character that Fr. Maydieu compared spiritually to those of matrimony. Members of the Order were to sally forth to show the various elements of the Resistance how to perfect their "mystiques" in the Uriage manner. Thus, high-level emissaries were dispatched to contact de Gaulle and "flying squadrons" into the countryside to guide the *maquis* so that their deficient mystiques could be "transcended spiritually" and "converge" in the construction of the better world of the personalist-Teilhardian Faith.

The enthusiasm with which this labor was undertaken was genuine, but especially so with respect to the Marxist component of the Resistance Movement. Many, if not perhaps most personalists, felt a preference for the vital energy of the Marxist-Leninist element in the United Nations Alliance. Despite the fact that its classic mishmash of Enlightenment mechanism and willfulness violated the basic Catholic understanding of man's simultaneously natural and supernatural, individual and social character, the Soviet communal emphasis was more immediately satisfying to the personalists' pronounced social sense. One sees this not only among members of the Order but also in the writings and labors of priests and bishops trying to understand the "mystique" of the proletariat in German labor camps and ordinary French factories. Systematic training for the latter purpose was offered, from 1943 onwards, under the patronage of the supra-diocesan *Mission de France*.

Uriage teachers were themselves deeply involved in these priestly activities. Fr. Dillard, for example, canonized the Soviet citizens he encountered in the labor camps and insisted that all industrial workers were born to carry out their tasks with the aid of specific virtues denied to other people. But an Uriage-like openness was noticeable in other, similar-minded circles. All such enthusiasts explained that there were "riches in modern disbelief, in atheist Marxism, for example, which are presently lacking to the fullness of the Christian conscience".[11] Enlightened spirits thus had "to share the faith in and the mystique of the Revolution and the Great Day (i.e., when all spiritually valid approaches would converge)",[12] as did one priest who asked to die "turned towards Russia, mother of the proletariat, as towards that mysterious homeland where the Man of the future is being forged".[13]

One major problem with this enthusiasm was that the Catholic peoples who ultimately came under Soviet control did not show themselves as open to the charms of Marxist-Leninist communal energy as its personalist supporters had done. Yes, a movement of so-called Pax Priests, with an underlying theme of shared Catholic and Marxist pathways to international harmony and social justice, eventually did develop. However, it was tainted by its association with the governments of the Peoples Republics and the practical material benefits that could be gained for its adherents through such an alliance. In general, the experience of Soviet Marxism-Leninism, linked as it was with the reality of a party dictatorship backed by the military strength of the Red Army, did not become popular with the believing Catholic masses. This was especially true in those post-war years when the Papacy vigorously preached an anti-communist message. Moreover, insofar as the Russian authorities did feel the need to cooperate with religious forces, they usually found attempts to collaborate with national Orthodox Churches simpler and more fruitful than efforts to manipulate an international Roman Catholicism. Rome was as resistant to the allurements of the Marxist Defender of the Peace as she had been to its imperial counterpart, promoted by Marsilius of Padua in medieval times.

Another difficulty with Marxist-Leninist communal energy was its closure to the crucial prophetic mission of the personalists. One must remember that the sons of Uriage always retained their

---

[11] Poulat, *Les prêtres-ouvrières* (Cerf, 1999), p. 408.
[12] Ibid., p. 386.
[13] Ibid., p. 244.

wartime sense of being a priestly nation, a people set apart, chosen to judge which aspects of burgeoning mystiques were and were not acceptable on the road to convergence. Marxism-Leninism, like fascism, was indeed acceptable in spirit. But it was acceptable as yet another "monstrous pre-figuration" of a happier future that had to be spiritually transcended in order to fulfill its true destiny. Uriage personalists were called upon to "witness" to the Marxist-Leninist "mystique" by raising it to a higher and fully appropriate level of consciousness — inside the Soviet Bloc as much as elsewhere.

Unfortunately, the Stalinist cult of personality, the omnipresence of the Red Army, and the jealous apparatchiks of the postwar era stood in the way of their prophetic vocation. Worse still, with the fall in 1964 of a highly anti-religious Nikita Khruschev who at least possessed the virtue of rocking the Soviet boat to promote the meritorious within the communist ranks, "security for the apparatchiks" became the primary goal of the whole of the shaken party membership. Hence, the growth of that pervasive cynicism that affected not only the Soviet population at large but the system's functionaries as well. For party functionaries understood that they survived as an elite only by demanding as little as possible in the way of labor, discipline, and the cultivation of "special virtues of the proletariat" from the common run of socialist mankind.

None of these realities meant that Marxism was no longer still worth "transcending"; only that different paths to ensuring fulfillment of the sacred socialist mission were required. Divergent paths would have to be found outside of the sphere of influence wherein ran the writ of the apparatchiks and the Red Army. Still, many other vital cultural forces, some of which had already begun to attract personalist attention before 1939, were manifesting their potential for mobilizing energetic mass support in more pronounced ways during the postwar era. Some of these, like the feminist and sexual liberation movement, were vigorous in the Western world. But, perhaps even more importantly, numerous other vital forces were to be found in the newly independent nations of Asia, Africa, and Oceania as well as in the semi-colonial protectorates of Latin America. Such energies reflected either flips on familiar European Enlightenment themes on the one hand or a resurgence of local, native beliefs and customs on the other.

Of course, all these vibrant developments of Western and indigenous cultures also desperately needed witness and prophetic transcending to ensure their perfection and ultimate convergence in the Holy Spirit. Latin America became particularly appealing to personalists and fellow travelers like Mounier, Chenu, Lebret, and even Maritain. Here, such men found social unrest in conjunction with an accelerated industrial development fueled by foreign capital, all of which seemed to portend the growth of a new and seemingly more "spirit-friendly" Marxism throughout the region. The energy unleashed by Fidel Castro (b. 1926) and Che Guevara (1928–1967) excited an especially explosive enthusiasm. Personalists thus began to hope that they would be able to use Latin America as a proving ground, diving into its "real world of the oppressed", giving testimony to its budding message of impatience and rage with "structures of sinful dependence", and rousing it to the kind of Marxist liberation that the Holy Spirit wanted but the apparatchiks of the Soviet Bloc stubbornly refused to permit. Yes, the mass of inert Latin American believers might not yet understand its own victimization — just as the bulk of Catholics had not grasped what the spiritually awakened Lamennais had to tell them. But that was always the job of the prophet: to shake a sleeping people out of its dogmatic slumbers to an appreciation of its true energy and the goal towards which it was unconsciously striving.

Dictatorial and aging apparatchiks were certainly an obstacle to the emergence of a better world, but they were not the only danger standing in the path of vital energies and their future convergence. Traditional Catholicism itself, which from Uriage days had "feared the insistence on bringing together men with different 'mystiques'", was increasingly seen to be at least as great a threat as an unresponsive Soviet Marxism, arousing in personalists "a 'manly' impatience with clericalism, dogma and the orthodox".[14] Catholic authoritarianism, manifested in its insistence upon adherence to frozen teachings and rituals, had to give way to changes dictated by diving into the living realities and vibrant energies of the day. Hence, the deeply committed Fr. Dillard ended by saying that his work in the vibrant forced labor factory was more important than his Mass, and, indeed, that the very machine on which he toiled itself actually had a soul of its own.

Mounier is particularly instructive with respect to this intensifying dismissal of the whole of the Church's traditional teaching and practice. His vision had always logically involved the possibility of shelving entire realms of Christian scripture, theology, and spirituality, should they clash with the "emerging convergence." By the last years of the war, "there was little place for sin, redemption and resurrection in the debate; the central acts of the Christian drama were set aside".[15] Nietzsche's critique of slavish Christianity now seemed to him to be unanswerable, and he "came to think that Roman Catholicism was an integral part of almost all he hated. Then, when he searched his soul, he discovered that the aspects of himself which he appreciated least were his 'Catholic' traits".[16] Doing what one willed was the *unum necessarium*. Not surprisingly, everything rational from the Greek tradition that had been used to support Christianity and dampen the vital will was execrated along with Catholicism as well. The Socratics, for him, were indeed Seeds of the Logos — and, as such, had to be driven into the wilderness with a fiery sword. Those obsessed with Catholic dogma, Catholic practice, and the philosophical hunt for the Logos all required diagnosis and serious psychiatric help.

[14] Hellman, *The Knight Monks*, p. 88.
[15] Hellman, *Mounier*, p. 255.
[16] Ibid., p. 190.

Hence, Mounier now flatly denounced old-fashioned Christianity and Christians. Christianity, he wrote, was "conservative, defensive, sulky, afraid of the future." Whether it "collapses in a struggle or sinks slowly in a coma of self-complacency," it was doomed. Christians were castigated, in Nietzschean style, as "these crooked beings who go forward in life only sidelong with downcast eyes, these ungainly souls, these weighers-up of virtues, these dominical victims, these pious cowards, these lymphatic heroes, these colourless virgins, these vessels of ennui, these bags of syllogisms, these shadows of shadows...".[17] Metaphysical speculation, Mounier declared, was a characteristic of "lifeless schizoid personalities."... He referred to intelligence and spirituality as "bodily diseases" and attributed the indecisiveness of many Christians to their ignorance of "how to jump a ditch or strike a blow." "Modern psychiatry," Mounier wrote, had shed light on the morbid taste for the "spiritual," for "higher things," for the ideal and for effusions of the soul... Thus, once again, he dismissed many forms of religious devotion as the result of psychosis, self-deception or vanity. Prayer was often a sign of psychological illness and weakness that analysis could do much to heal. Vigorous exercise would help as well.[18]

This brings us back to the liturgical question, the liturgy obviously being one of the most important aspects of daily Christian life that would have to change with the emergence of a new and more vital personalist order. Uriage recognized as much, and was therefore permeated by the spirit of "pastoral concern" characterizing the more recent liturgical movement. This movement, in fact, was formative in shaping its own understanding of the importance and methodology of accommodation to active "mystiques" for the sake of the creation of the self-sacrificing individuals that true personhood required.

[17] Hellman, *Mounier*, p. 191.
[18] Ibid., pp. 192–193.

Fr. Maydieu was already active before the war, together with "friends of *Sept*", celebrating new style Masses, during which the priest faced the people and provided a French narration.[19] Fr. Doncoeur, terrified that vital life was passing inert Catholics by, became enthusiastic for pastoral liturgical developments in Germany as early as 1923. He used the model of games and sports events, along with the general desire of youth to cooperate as a group, to guide the French scouting movement down a new liturgical direction:[20]

> Games can also be an excellent preparation for worship, which to the little ones appears to be very little different from a game. This should not scandalize us. The word game is not in the child's vocabulary, and particularly in the realm of scouting, it is a synonym for diversion. A game is an action, passionate insofar as it is sincerely played. Well, official worship is eminently sincere. Children sense this. They find satisfaction in this atmosphere of truth. They savor this serious action, wherein all participate, body and soul, this collective and ordained action, similar in nature to those grand modern sports events wherein modern youth finds its discipline and sometimes its mystique. But the little faithful heart senses well that worship is more noble than sports. Worship is the Big Game, the Sacred Game which is being played for the Chief of Chiefs.... Among the troops the Mass is generally a Dialogue Mass at which all actively participate. Certain among them make the offering. The cadets which Father Doncoeur leads each summer with knapsacks across France's roads also have the Dialogue Mass. Gathered before the altar, they respond to the liturgical prayers, make the offering of the host which will be consecrated for them at the Offertory....

[19] J. Duquesne, quoted in D. Bonneterre, *Le mouvment liturgique* (Fideliter), p. 39.
[20] Bonneterre, p. 38.

Concerned as it was with using all communal tools to build persons possessing the "leadership mystique", Uriage turned the entire day into a "manly" liturgical experience. Bonfires were lit, backs slapped, virile poems and hymns composed, and special pageants mounted. Uriage claimed that all of these were, of course, inspired by "deep feeling," constituting demands upon the developing persons of the community, rejection of which would have been a breach of *Volksgemeinschaft* equivalent to an individualist sin against the Holy Spirit. Interestingly enough, all of this new, "natural", participatory, creative — and expensive — liturgical life was being elaborated while Frs. Maydieu, Doncoeur, Chenu, Congar and others were bringing into existence what would be the extremely influential "Center for Pastoral Liturgy", designed to effect similar changes in ordinary ecclesiastical life.

Worker-Marxist-Soviet mania from 1942 onwards increased the reformers demand for a liturgy based upon a pastoral response to particular mystiques to fever pitch. This often played upon Pius XII's well-known willingness to take risks on the pastoral level if real success could be demonstrated to emerge from them. In any case, Henri Godin's (1906–1944) famous work, *France: Pays de Mission?* (1943), outlining worker dechristianization, had created a sense of crisis in France that the pope could perhaps be counted upon to take seriously. This book argued that the loss of Church influence among the working class was so dire that all prudence had to be tossed aside. Lack of any precise plan for how to guide the pressing need to dive into the worker mystique was attributed to the spontaneous genius of those participating in the program and their unfailing faith in the Holy Spirit.

One thing alone was certain: the liturgy and the priesthood were out of sync with the vital world of the laboring man. All that was associated with what Paul Claudel disparagingly called the "mass with one's back to the people" had therefore to be abandoned.[21] Such a mass had become the precious toy of little minds and bigots who could not understand the New Order emerging around them. Hence, also, the critique of Fr. Dillard, who dismissed any supposed difficulties emerging from a total rejection of an anachronistic Catholic priestly mission. He insisted that his worker clientele would be able to sense the superior spirituality of what others might be tempted to call a secularized clergy due to a *je ne sais quoi* emanating from its own fresh sacerdotal mystique:[22]

> My Latin, my liturgy, my mass, my prayer, my sacerdotal ornaments, all of that made me a being apart, a curious phenomenon, something like a (Greek) pope or a Japanese bonze, of whom there remain still some specimen, provisionally, while waiting for the race to die out.
>
> Religion as they [the workers] knew it is a type of bigotry for pious women and chic people served by disguised characters who are servants of capitalism.... If we succeed in ridding our religion of the unhealthy elements that encumber it, petty superstitions, the bourgeois "go to Mass" hypocrisy, etc. we will find easily with the Spirit of Christ the mystique which we need to reestablish our homeland.

Yes, there was no doubt that the constraints of traditional Catholicism had to be relaxed, along with those of nefarious Soviet apparatchik influences, if the good spirits of Marxism and other energetic movements in Europe and the Third World were to come to fruition and converge. But how, practically speaking, could this work of liberation be accomplished? The only other viable political and social vision was that of American pluralism, and this outlook

---

[21] Cholvy and Hilaire, *Jeunesses chrétiennes au xxe siècle* (Ouvrières, 1991), III, 274.
[22] Poulat, *Les prêtres-ouvrières*, pp. 329, 333.

did not at first appear to many personalists to be all that promising. "The Americans," Beuve-Mery, who went from Uriage to the management of the highly influential postwar French newspaper, *Le Monde*, complained, "could prevent us from carrying out the obligatory revolution, and their materialism does not even have the tragic grandeur of the materialism of the totalitarians".[23]

Still, a number of personalist fellow travelers, Jacques Maritain prominent among them, were much more hopeful, arguing that American pluralism was an immensely powerful revolutionary force suitable for breaking down many petrified tradition — if only it were witnessed to properly. Through the Marshall Plan and its support for supra-national, continental economic reconstruction, pluralism's powerful vision had already begun to break down traditional authorities and work for that European union that so many personalists — along with the Nazi New Order itself — had also longed to achieve. Maritain argued that American pluralism might even lend itself to a convergence with the most vital spiritual elements of a Marxism whose true transcendent mission was being botched by the Soviets.

Besides, one simply could not deny that the impact of the pluralist message of a practical openness to a world of diversity was as strong on European Catholics as it was on everyone else on the war-weary Continent. They, too, were tired of a divisiveness that had seemingly produced nothing but hatred and conflict. The words of the conqueror were beautiful words indeed, and Maritain could point to the fact that American Catholics were among their most fervent propagandists. Pluralism could become *the* Defender of the Peace and *the* Defender of Freedom for everything and everyone, including fresh, exciting, energetic developments noticeable in the Old as well as the New and Third Worlds. It could, therefore, powerfully aid the work of personalists in witnessing to their many vital mystiques and assuring their convergence in fulfillment of the

---

[23] Hellman, *The Knight Monks*, p. 213.

message of the Holy Spirit. Perhaps. But, once again, the Holy Spirit in question was one whose teaching would have been recognizable to Lamennais, and, in one way or another, to supporters of the whole "tradition" of Gnosticism, Nominalism, the Reformation, and the Enlightenment, from whose decadent path to "purification" the Catholic revival movement of the nineteenth century had passionately sought to remove the Church in her Head and Members.

C. DIVING INTO THE PLURALIST MYSTIQUE AND THE SUICIDE OF CATHOLICISM

For what, exactly, would "diving into" the "mystique" of pluralism actually entail? The best way to begin to give an answer to this question is by briefly expounding upon what we have already learned about pluralism's Americanist childhood: namely, that the American message to the world means more than what its simple words of "peace" and "freedom" *seem* on the surface to indicate; it also means everything that comes along with these words in its historical and sociological baggage train.

In practice, diving into pluralism's "lived reality" signifies immersion in the experience and teaching of the first important society in the western world that never knew a stage of orthodox Christianity. It necessitates becoming one with a culture deeply influenced by the atomist doctrine of total depravity and the effects of its secularization on the one hand and by the desires of the founding moderate Whig Enlightenment oligarchy and their consequences on the other. It then entails praising what emerges from this union *both* as a purely pragmatic tool for providing a tranquil, free, prosperous social order in a multicultural America *as well as* a sacred, providential gift of God, destined for missionary transport everywhere around the globe; a new and more divine *thesis*.

American pluralism thus brings with it experience of the full development of the initial Protestant animus against a blasphemous, tyrannical, fleshly, Word-drenched Church. That animus, expanded through secularization beyond its original anti-Roman focus, gradually manifested itself in an attack upon all authoritative institutions providing guidance for individual human action. It came to see in the American system a ticket to an atomistic Eden where the "unbound rhinoceros" could pursue his personal agenda without fear of condemnation from Faith, Reason, or his equally liberated neighbors. Hence, diving into this lived reality means approval of "unbinding the rhinoceros".

But becoming one with the American mystique also brings with it experience of the full development of the moderate, Whig Enlightenment ideal. That form of the Enlightenment sought a civil order ruled over by a weak State. This weakness permitted satisfaction of the material interests of the dominant elements in private society. Such domination began with an oligarchy whose conservatism also led it to preserve a traditional language of respect for a Christian-sounding God—who respected the need to keep His distance from daily human affairs. Diving into this lived reality means justifying satisfaction of the material wishes of the strongest unbound rhinoceros in society as an integral part of mankind's last, best hope for maintaining a peace and freedom in accord with both common sense and God's Providence.

Still, the Whiggish passion for maintaining civil order was forced to work together with the radical dedication to pursuit of an atomist freedom. And that more radical fervor was itself, in turn, constrained to take the much more conservative moderate Enlightenment tendency seriously. These two concerns proved to influence one another, guaranteeing the development of the system in a way that both changed and yet confirmed the founding oligarchy's original designs. It is necessary to examine this two-fold effect before the picture of the lived reality of the American experience and the consequences of diving into it is complete.

America changed in that the Founders' conviction that they could maintain the dominance of the existing propertied Whig elite as an obvious dictate of both common sense and God's Providence proved to be misplaced. John Locke's principle of toleration — with its "multiplication of factions" to a degree that would render any community or coalition of forces that might try to threaten the power of the original revolutionary planter-merchant oligarchy impotent to effect real change — was indeed supposed to work on its behalf. But the radical conception of the meaning of American freedom, in practice, gave to societies and individuals prepared to do whatever was necessary to satisfy their own ideas and material desires the chance to expand the borders of what eighteenth century men said that common sense signified and permitted. Growing insistence upon the need for openness rendered it progressively more difficult to "close" the vision of "freedom" and "common sense" within more limited Moderate Enlightenment bounds and take its notion of God's "natural law" seriously. A development of visions of radical freedom increasingly blocked appeal to any faith-filled or rational standard for judging the validity, justice, and prudence of any desire or action of any specific group or individual. The path to replacement of the existing elite was simply to use one's freedom more willfully than the Founders had conceived possible. This allowed a new community or individual to become so significant and powerful as to require "integration" of its concerns into the syllabus of ideas and behavior patterns deemed acceptable by the existing establishment if only for the sake of peace and quiet. But such a fresh and still more "unbound rhinoceros" could itself come to dominate society and define anew what God, common sense, "the will of the Founders", toleration, peace, and progress meant. The civil religion could be counted upon to drill in the argument that a universal liberty continued to triumph under the orderly domination of the new and still more arbitrary elite. Some of its own members might even honestly believe this tale of a unique, simultaneous American guarantee of peace and freedom to represent the truth.

Despite the change of personnel, however, the kind of order favored by the founding oligarchy—an order permitting the tranquil enjoyment of material desires and possession, free from the unwanted interference of a dogmatic Church and a powerful State—was to an overwhelming degree confirmed under all subsequent elites. Those strong conservative influences whose passion for order allowed for the integration of new elements into existing society continued to be exerted and have an enormous impact. Such influences, as always, urged everyone to renounce the private use of political freedom to shape the public society in which men lived according to particular spiritual and intellectual convictions. For the men of order argued that it was precisely such attempts to unify thought and action that had been the historical cause of horrible division and bloody disturbances of the peace.

Concerns for the maintenance of public peace in a country promoting a radical freedom increased exponentially due to the multicultural waves of migrants arriving in the United States from 1848 onwards. A Protestant rooted America found the path to unity in the midst of such diversity through an anchoring in the one characteristic every fallen man shared in common: Original Sin. Free citizens were to be unified through a systematic exploitation of the common fallen human passion for willful satisfaction of material desires. The result was that Americans learned that they were really expected to use their liberty in but one single, concupiscent fashion--for the attainment and protection of material possessions. In other words, even though the theoretical freedom granted to communities and individuals under the American pluralist "mystique" was one allowing them to "be themselves" and potentially even to "go wild", in practice, that freedom became a liberty merely to hunt for and protect property in a myriad of communal and personal fashions. This reductionist freedom, based upon promoting the chief consequence of Original Sin, then had to be praised as the greatest gift to the human mind, heart, and soul known to history. Whether that gift was granted by God or nature was left to individual taste to determine — but not to impose upon others.

Strong and unscrupulous men whose eyes were open gradually realized that the "even-handed" American pluralist methodology put them in a position "freely" to create a public "order" in which they devoured the weak. Once again, this could, theoretically, be done in the name of an ideology, but the tendency of the system was to create an order based upon a materialist expression of strength and willfulness. And the logic of this tendency was to degenerate and ensure construction of an order based upon the dictates of ever more willful libertine or criminal strongmen. All these strongmen maintained their alliance with honest American pluralist ideologues who did not realize that they were being "mugged" by their own beloved system. They also allied their cause with that of dishonest rhetorical word merchants who made their living by justifying and ennobling the oppression of the weak and the gullible, exploiting the powerful American civil religion and its images to ease their labors. It was all these developments that guaranteed that the system "spiraled downwards", ending in that boring, materialist, intellectually barren sameness — that "tumultuous monotony" — depicted by the nineteenth century Catholic activist Louis Veuillot as a chief characteristic of the coming, global "Empire of the World".

Communities and individuals resisting the lived reality of the American system could — and did — hold back the logic of its growth and development. But those who "dived into" its "mystique" to help to bring it to its perfection assisted in unleashing its full fury. They, at best, would end by embracing a thoughtless, soulless, materialist existence; one wherein the dance of life, with all of its many spiritual and intellectually difficult problems, would come to a halt. In other words, at best, the truly law-abiding pluralist minded community or individual would commit spiritual and intellectual suicide. For this is what the pluralist Defender of the Peace ultimately demanded of men—although from the lawmaker's standpoint the action performed should more properly be labeled euthanasia rather than suicide. Having "dived into" the lived American reality, they could only use their freedom either to praise the privilege that they had been given to live their lives serving the material interests of the current masters of the system or, worse still, to dominate society by playing this materialist game still better than their opponents.

All modern proponents of Protestant and Enlightenment "freedom" insist that a new age of Reason and Liberty dawned for mankind with the return to the proper understanding of "nature as is" promoted by the Renaissance and the Reformation. Anyone who questions this glorious victory is answered not by rational argument but with haughty condescension. He is condemned as an enemy of God and man, and one who lacks that faith in Progress that is urgently required to assure the full development of a *novus ordo saeclorum*.

American pluralism and its Divine Republic continue this "tradition" with a special vengeance and a particular success. Nevertheless, they sow the wind with their dogma of a pragmatic and order-friendly openness to freedom and diversity. In consequence, they reap the whirlwind of impassioned, irrational, willful dominance over the truly serious and peaceful man. Abandoning God's Law and Reason, the civilization they produce has nothing left to restrain it. And yet the irony is, as Louis Veuillot noted, that those who consider themselves the victors and the rulers of this civilization cannot even sin with any real gusto. It is a cheapened, inhuman way of life in arid suburban shopping malls and freeways to nowhere that stirs their ambitions and libido. Every aspect of modernity smacks of death. It was fitting, therefore, that American pluralism should arise to give to modernity a thoroughgoing culture of living death—a living euthanasia—to sate its thirst for eternal slumber.

Conquered peoples, as Horace noted, have sometimes taken their captors captive. But not all conquerors are Romans, and frequently the consequences can be quite different. The vanquished can come to adopt their conquerors' language, customs, heroes, and religions as their own. Indeed, they can reach the point of recoiling in horror at the mere mention of their earlier beliefs and ancient champions. Barring this, they can end up forgetting them entirely and even denying that they ever existed. This cultural conquest can have certain positive effects when the victor is something or someone better than the vanquished. We are rightly edified, as was St. Ambrose, at the contemplation of ancient Rome, humble enough to surrender her gods and a number of her traditional customs, once conquered by the superior truth of the Word Incarnate. We can rejoice at the thought of a powerful tribe like that of the Franks under Clovis, abandoning itself to its Roman and Catholic cultural conquerors and forsaking its pagan barbarism in consequence. But we should be saddened whenever we encounter a high civilization, heir to the most profound truths and cultural achievements, which so learns to adore a debased conqueror that it voluntarily silences the songs of the glories of its own princes, warriors, and thinkers. We should be saddened when it no longer recognizes its former accomplishments or beliefs when confronted with them, and even uses the arguments of its masters to eclipse them further.

Contemporary Catholic civilization throughout the Western world, and the Catholic peoples who benefited from it, fit into this second and truly pathetic category of the conquered. In our day, the vast majority of Catholics, clerics and laymen alike, consciously or unconsciously, fall on their knees daily only to commit religious and cultural suicide. They recite the tawdry slogans of their conquerors, beg instruction in their masters' religion and customs, and burn incense before a host of "heroes" who are non-Catholic at best and vehement enemies of the Christian God and man at worst. Although the demoralization leading to this dreadful reality has been very long in preparation, it is only recently that we have seen such mass hara-kiri actually performed in public. This ignoble defeat, as T. S. Eliot lamented of the destruction of modern man as a whole, has been achieved "not with a bang, but a whimper".

The Second Vatican Council proved to be the tool—not the prime cause, but the chief tool—through which the conqueror imposed his marching orders upon the Mystical Body of Christ. Pope John XXIII's Council ensured that Catholic personalists and their allies, taking advantage of the pluralist spirit sweeping the Western world due to the victory of the United States in the Second World War—and the pressure employed to maintain it afterwards—could seize control of the powerful machinery of the Universal Church. Having done so, they then encouraged a Catholicism that "gave witness" to various vital energies. These ranged from Marxism to the final logical expressions of the moral and materialist visions of the Enlightenment, both Radical and Moderate, to Latin American Liberation Theology, and to Third World religions—in short, to anything "strong", whose inevitable "convergence" in fulfillment of the "plan" of the Holy Spirit had to be prepared by men who believed themselves to possess a prophetic vision.

The result has been the greatest disaster for the spread of the corrective and transforming message of the Word in history. That message, the *only* truly different, vital, energetic force in human life, was the one force that these prophets of the Spirit would not permit to have further impact within a camp of the saints whose consciousness had been raised. They would not allow such an impact because it seriously *could* and *must* change man and society. Hence, the conquest of the Church and Catholics by the Grand Coalition of the Status Quo, its word merchants, and its program on behalf of "business as usual" demands of "nature as is" leading to the triumph of the strongest wills was prepared. Hence, the "spiraling downwards" of control of the Catholic world into ever more ideologically insane, libertine, or criminal hands was assured.

And, sad to say, clergy and laity alike enthusiastically praised this disaster all the while that its dreadful consequences were painfully manifesting themselves.

Let me hasten to add that I am by no means arguing that the Church would have been in magnificent shape should the Second Vatican Council never have occurred. Her ecclesiology and her understanding of her true strength as Christ continued in time were still not rigorous enough for that to be true. Readers will remember that many disputes over ecclesiological problems had emerged after 1563. These disputes had not been resolved at Trent and they were in no way fully thrashed out at Vatican I in 1870 either. It is hard to see how almost any specific issue emerging in the 1960s would have surprised the controversialists of the previous four hundred years. The papal-episcopal college question, Church-State relations, the advisability of liturgical changes that included the use of the vernacular, and the need for a clearer teaching on the full meaning of the sacrament of matrimony were all matters familiar to past disputants. The only way for much of this discussion to appear unusual is to think that Trent and Vatican One pronounced dogmatically on more matters than they actually did. Many Catholics certainly believed this to have been the case. Thus, when the present crisis began, they were woefully mistaken regarding exactly what the definition of Papal Infallibility did and did not demand of them in the way of faithful obedience.

Moreover, we have seen that the Church was experiencing "dangers on all fronts", making any move to deal with one dilemma an invitation for another to take shape and dominate the future course of events. Many Catholics did not respond to these dangers in a balanced fashion that was open to the fullness of the message of the Word in history. And even though Church authorities, highly alarmed over the situation created by a general European loss of faith, had made preparations for the shift of the center of gravity of Christianity to other continents, it was inevitable that their laudable work brought still further confusion and missteps in its train. But all of this was noticeable before 1962, and was merely exacerbated by the Council.[24]

On the procedural level, the disastrous developments briefly outlined above must be ascribed to the Second Vatican Council's failure to follow the wisdom of Trent. Trent, the reader will recall, had opted for a simultaneous treatment of pastoral and doctrinal questions, even in the face of tremendous pressure to ignore the latter. It had sound reasons for making this choice, given the fact that powerful new heretical forces were highly active in contemporary Europe and ready to shape any purely "pastoral" decisions to fit their packed doctrinal program. Doctrinal clarity gave Trent a much more solid control over pastoral initiatives.

But we have seen that erroneous beliefs and ideologies merely increased in number and violence over the following centuries. If anything, what might not have been as clear more than four centuries earlier, ought to have been absolutely transparent by the 1960s: namely, that a "pragmatic" policy that did not address real, existing, powerful divisions of belief could easily lead to the triumph of hidden doctrines promoted by determined minorities. Nineteenth century intransigents had warned that anyone who failed to appreciate the errors of the modern definition of freedom and tried to act "pragmatically" on the basis of its teaching would drag what was, in historical fact, a weak Church into a "free" and "open" co-existence and competition with immensely willful and strong enemies. And, under such conditions, she was, at least humanly speaking, bound to lose. Such "pragmatism" would, in reality, be tantamount to tempting Providence.

---

[24] For the Council, see J.M. Mayeur, ed. Histoire du Christianisme (Desclée, Thirteen Volumes, 1990–2002), XIII, 21–111; H. Jedin and J. Dolan, History of the Church (Crossroads, Ten Volumes, 1981), X, 96–151; Y. Chiron, *Paul VI* (Perrin, 1993), pp. 168–251; R. Wiltgen, *The Rhine Flows into the Tiber* (Tan, 1967); M. Davies, *Liturgical Revolution* (Angelus, Three Volumes, 1987), II (*Pope John's Council*).

A *Catholic* pragmatism, one that was dictated by the message of the Word Incarnate, recognized the central importance of doctrinal clarity, authoritatively taught, in defending the only truth that could honestly set men free. It understood just how much weak, struggling, sinful human beings needed all the concrete assistance they could get in order to grasp the fullness of truth and to do what was right and necessary for both their earthly happiness and their eternal salvation. Accordingly, it preached the obligation to correct and transform human societies and institutions so that they themselves would embody and teach sound natural and supernatural lessons. The omnipotent God could indeed protect the Church within a "free market place of ideas and life styles", where truth was accorded no privileged place among the seductive and often violent advertising of ideological commodities. But He would do so through the heroic sufferings of His faithful and not through the merits of the personalist or pluralist "method". A true Catholic pragmatism could not legitimately force believers into the spiritual equivalent of a game of poker with a team of card sharks and then blithely demand supernatural intervention from God to protect them. What one was likely to get, in consequence, was a new but disguised dogmatic teaching, uniting the Church with the State and the world more tightly than thinkers from Marsilius of Padua to Lamennais could ever have dreamed possible.

Still, even though Trent's reasons for rejecting a purely pastoral approach towards dealing with problems within the universal Church were as valid as ever, and the intransigents had identified further grounds for following in its footsteps, the anti-dogma camp had also gained many new adherents in the intervening period. Trent's own emphasis on the importance of demonstrating practical success had helped to give "pragmatic-minded" prelates, priests, and lay activists some justification in the decades and centuries following its closure. Students of Church History in general, and readers of this essay in particular, know that these "pragmatists" came to include Jansenists, Mennaisians, liberal Catholics, modernists, and personalists. Numerous pressing scientific, political, and social changes exposing gaps—if not errors—in the Church's corrective and transforming labors also worked to bring pastoral matters to the forefront of many faithful and concerned Catholics' minds and hearts. In short, "pastoral" became a "good word" whose recitation could cover a multitude of treasonous acts, sins, and doctrinal stupidities.

The post-war climate of opinion offered the "purely pastoral" camp its latest and most powerful source of support. Taking advantage of the *Zeitgeist,* a partisan organizational talent that had gone from strength to strength since the end of the First World War, and a powerful sense of mission, the personalist-pluralist alliance steered the Second Vatican Council away from the much more Tradition-friendly methodology its original program envisioned. Instead of a Tridentine-inspired, joint dogmatic-pastoral approach, a purely pastoral language and strategy was adopted. This ended by serving the cause of the willful manipulators of freedom and the word merchants profiting from their custom. In the name of a practical, pragmatic openness to understanding and dealing with the new and diverse needs of "modern man", the inevitable happened. The Council proceeded to confront a host of problems on the basis of a personalist and pluralist definition of what the words "pastoral" and "pragmatic" meant. And we have now clearly seen that this definition works in union with a vision of nature, man, and freedom that are not only different from traditional Catholic teachings on the subject, but also totally destructive to the corrective and transforming message of the Word in history.

The Second Vatican Council as such could not and did not claim to act infallibly once it specifically proclaimed its intention to deal with issues on the pastoral as opposed to the doctrinal plane. Therefore, it could only bind consciences to those of its edicts that actually recalled already known teachings on faith and morals. Unfortunately, however, the personalist-pluralist victors at the Council had as little interest in the substantive teaching of the "old" Magisterium regarding infallibility as on any other subject. Their concern was simply how the principle of infallibility could practically be used to promote their agenda. Joining together to interpret the Council's "spirit", they were happy to play upon believers' respect for the traditional teaching Church to give to what were purely pastoral decisions the aura of dogmatic pronouncements—more than that, the *sole* dogmatic pronouncements that modern Catholics were obliged to heed and obey in the future. Hence, the victory of a powerful faction serving an ideology blessing an irrational mindlessness was unjustifiably cloaked with the authority of the Holy Spirit—that same Holy Spirit whose infallible doctrinal guidance was at first rejected, lest it manifest the intolerant, closed, and pastorally divisive behavior that authoritative direction was chastised for displaying in the past.

Moreover, the fideism underlying the personalist and pluralist mentality choked a true Catholic inquiry into this mysterious return of the Holy Spirit from exile, just as it choked a true examination of anything else that happened at the Council. Instead, it used its usurped magisterial role to demand Catholic recitation of the usual slogans regarding the need for pragmatism, openness, freedom, and peace as an alternative to serious Faith and Reason. Harping on its mandate from the Holy Spirit, it then tossed to the winds that entire corpus of nineteenth and twentieth-century theological, philosophical, political, historical, psychological, and sociological wisdom that had painstakingly analyzed exactly why such pastoral methodology could only end in a willful assault upon the full message of the Word in history. It ignored the fact that such pastoral methodology had actually already engaged in a similar assault once before, in the eighteenth century. Along with this wisdom went the guidance of the Church Fathers, previous ecumenical gatherings, the decisions of nearly two millennia of Popes, the canonical tradition, and everything else that could be cited to understand the extent of the Council's authority or put it into its proper historical and dogmatic perspective. The conquerors of the Council insisted that a failure to heed their interpretation of its decisions, if not a sign of insanity pure and simple, could not signify anything other than a stubborn closure of one's heart to the triumphant judgment of the Holy Spirit. In short, the triumph of openness was celebrated by shutting the door imperiously on the whole teaching of the Word Incarnate in history and the Seeds of the Logos harmonized together with it. "Words" alone were allowed to proclaim the Incarnate Word; words that servants of "nature as is", from Isocrates to Marsilius of Padua and beyond, would have much appreciated — and similarly abused.

Before moving on, let us remember that another extremely dangerous contemporary accusation lurked behind every attack upon a critic's stubborn closing of his heart to the will of this new kind of Holy Spirit: namely, his possession of a "fascist mentality". The fascist label was used as an effective club to brutalize and silence any and all criticism. The outside secular world, ecstatic over the Council's acceptance of the reigning *Zeitgeist*, joined in the rhetorical game, with the late Pope Pius XII turned into the symbol of an evil fascist spirit still festering in the bosom of the Catholic beast. Ironically, a Church that had been consistently chastised for the slightest interference in the realm of the State was thereby proclaimed guilty of not having interfered enough, at least where the Nazis were concerned, and of continuing to harbor villains justifying this unforgivable failure of ecclesiastical responsibility in her sacred precincts. The agents of a purge deemed to be essential to the restoration of Church health were personalists who, more than anyone else, had themselves nurtured a philo-fascist outlook in the interwar period. And, sadly, all this was to prove to serve a new and global unity of Church and State, designed to ensure the "public order" dear to the hearts of legalists of all previous ages on the basis of a religion submissive to the demands of "nature as is" alone.

Pity the poor opponent of the "Spirit of Vatican Two" who wanders into the realm of the post-conciliar personalist interpreting the infallible Magisterium of the Catholic Church! He is like someone going to a dinner party given by a man who had declared cannibalism to be the expression of his and all his other guests' deepest spiritual longing. Terrified at the thought of taking exception to his host's proclivity lest he be identified as an unrealistic, shriveled-up, anti-social individualist lacking faith in the action of the Spirit — and a fascist to boot — the poor soul will be eaten alive; devoured, ironically, at the command of the only *true* representative of the principle of the Triumph of the Will who is present. At least the victim can console himself with the thought that he is not alone in his misery. The same fate befell all of the teaching tools of the Mystical Body of Christ; all the teaching tools, and Catholics in the United States, Europe, and the Third World along with them.

Needless to say, such a revolution required a massive weakening of all existing Church teaching authorities and Catholic pastoral initiatives working to correct and transform the world in Christ.[25] Every thought and action of every pontiff, council, curial office, bishop, priest, religious, and faithful could now boldly be criticized by the infallible heralds of the Holy Spirit — Stalinists in Catholic garb — whose own judgments could, by definition, never be brought into question. The rhetoricians of the movement promoted this critical weakening of the Church's administration and heritage at the Council and in its aftermath through the Press, the numerous organizations lobbying for change in Rome, and the "experts", the *periti*, who served as the spokesmen for the winning faction's prominent bishops. All these forces, together, cited conciliar documents such as the pastoral Constitution, *Gaudium et*

---

[25] For the below, see Mayeur, XIII, 112–341; Jedin and Dolan, X, 96–177; Chiron, *Paul VI*, pp. 253–344.

Spes, as well as the Declaration on Religious Liberty, as proof that the Church was now committed to working together with broad "human values" that taught her "signs of the times" requiring neither censure nor ecclesiastical guidance. Post-conciliar committees did especially yeoman service in carrying out the task of dismantling and destruction. They continued to utter the voice of the Holy Spirit in slogan after slogan, mantra after mantra, as they sucked out whatever traditional substance could legitimately be found in the now "dogmatic" pastoral decrees and refilled them with suggestions for a renewal in line with the *Zeitgeist*. Replacement of appreciation for dogmatic truth by an openness to substance-free sloganeering was essential for the creation of that false "pilgrim spirit" ready to accept everything that the prophets of the here and now presented to the orphaned "People of God", without the slightest pretense of its Catholic correction and transformation.

Of all the doctrines that had to disappear, those of the Mystical Body of Christ and Christ as King of the universe were symbolically the most important. Both, together, emphasized much too clearly the direct connection of the Church with the Word Incarnate, her fleshly character as an organized society, and the practical effect that Christ's appearance in history must have on man and all of nature. Both, together, forced society to seek to organize itself according to "the common good" rather than whatever "worked" to provide "public order". The term "People of God", stripped free of any of its more traditional interpretations and loaded down with Ockhamite, Mennaisien, personalist, and pluralist meaning, gave to the Church that democratic atmosphere in which modern factions have most effectively worked to enforce their will on their undiscerning and self-immolating victims.

Such essential changes of emphasis on the doctrinal level were accompanied by a retreat from the ultramontanist-inspired, papal-centered administration of the Universal Church favored since the second half of the nineteenth century. This was exchanged for a "collegial" approach to ecclesiastical governance, one that sought to hand greater power over to national episcopacies and local ordinaries. But these latter forces had proven themselves historically to be much more vulnerable to narrow secular pressure and self-interested factions than the Papacy. In consequence, the ever-more self-confident personalist and pluralist interpreters of the now painfully hyperactive "Holy Spirit" could control their decisions even more effectively. The natural human values these prophets promoted were identified as the ones that the bishops and the Spirit Himself preferred — to the detriment of the other members of the Blessed Trinity and the Church's Magisterium as a whole. Ecclesiastical government thus fell from episcopal as well as papal hands. Constant papal traveling added to the destruction of normal administrative activity. It kept "the cat" so busy planning, taking, and assessing pastoral visits — along with potentially bankrupting the dioceses to which he traveled — that "the mice" could play at their massive work of dismantling the past and substituting the guidance of approved "natural energies" virtually undisturbed.

Meanwhile, traditional disciplines designed for the formation of Catholic theologians and philosophers, beginning with speculative theology and ending, ultimately, even with Holy Scripture itself, were swiftly emasculated as well, discredited as "contingent, outside forces" weighing down upon the energies of the present moment. Submission to such vital signs of the time promised a bright new day "when all will prophesy" with the spirit of "immediacy" of the first Christians. "Real world" problems, "felt reality", "contextualization", "the kerygma of travel", and other slogans that storytellers of past eras would have envied inventing were dinned into the ears of seminarians, students, and congregations to the confusion of the faithful and the enhancement of the power of the servants of "nature as is" inside the Church. And these slogans were destined to change whenever the Roman, national, diocesan, and parish committees of personalist and pluralist experts that equated their voices with that of the Holy Spirit felt the need for new, prophetic bumper stickers to cement their hold on an "energetic People of God" unfailingly commanded to keep still, be silent, and obey.

D. DESTRUCTION OF THE CATHOLIC LITURGY

Before moving on to discuss the effects of this weakening of Church authority on the political and social environment that reformers of all past ages saw to be of such great importance to the substantive labor of correction and transformation in Christ, let us first turn our attention to its impact upon the public prayer life of the Catholic world. For, as we have repeatedly reiterated, the daily worship of the Church is undoubtedly the most crucial of all the tools required for telling the varied members of the Mystical Body of Christ a good story about the true story of the Faith and its consequences for man and nature.[26]

This tale, the traditional liturgy told in a truly Word-friendly fashion. That liturgy was aimed entirely towards the worship of the Almighty and "seeing things" through His eyes. The most obvious sign of this orientation was its guidance by a priest who — *pace* Claudel — "did not turn his back on God". In relating its story about things divine, the traditional liturgy consistently focused upon the central truth that mankind can only understand life and fulfill its real promise by means of a total subordination to the Trinity and its plan for Creation. Yet, just as the Father sent the Son for our Redemption, that same God-centered liturgy also identified man's mission to nurture the whole of his created environment in order to gain its assistance in aiming his mind and heart to all the

---

[26] For the following, see Davies, *Liturgical Revolution*, I (*Cranmer's Godly Order*) and III (*Pope Paul's New Mass*); K. Gamber, *The Reform of the Roman Liturgy: Its Problems and Background* (Una Voce, 1993); D. von Hildebrand, *Liturgy and Personality* (Longmans, 1943).

perfect gifts that only come from above, from Divine Light. In fulfillment of this mission, Catholics put all of the magnificent tools of nature to use in God's worship, and with a rational and classical respect for the hierarchy of values in the process.

The holistic traditional liturgy then reinforced Catholic men in their mission regarding all the rest of their temporal activity. Believers left Holy Mass awakened to the Divine Light and to God's grace. They therefore expected to see the whole of nature used, liturgically, to tell a good story that pressed them onwards to understand and fulfill the goal of the entirety of existence. Regularly awakened to the value of each and every aspect of nature in the service of God through exposure to the traditional liturgy, believers readily understood that they required the aid of authoritative communities as well as aesthetic tools. For, despite what those who wished to leave the individual naked and exposed to the Triumph of the Will might argue, serious disciples of the Word recognized that human beings did not reach "adulthood" through liberation from their various natural "structures of dependence". Truly awakened Catholics grasped the importance of employing the authoritative labors of as many of these structures of dependence as they possibly could find, because all were a positive stimulus to a full grasp of reality and to proper, effective human action.

Moreover, they recognized that none of these natural tools could ever be rejected in the name of the "sea change" promised by preachers of an immediate apocalypse or millennium; that none became superfluous due to the arrival of some fresh, charismatic guide. None of these tools could be rejected due to having reached a "higher consciousness" as interpreted by prophetic voices that were not those of Christ's Church. True students of the Word, enlightened by a liturgy that focused them on the riches of God rather than passing parochial enthusiasms, realized that all natural aids to human knowledge and action would always be necessary, each and every one, and this until the end of time — so long, that is to say, as they accepted the corrective and transformative ministrations of Christ; and so long as believers stood on constant guard against their sinful misuse of all such gracious gifts of God.

Turn of the century modernism may have failed chiefly because of its exaggeratedly intellectual character. If reformers were to have a renewed opportunity to reshape the Church, they were indeed well advised to go about their business through the more powerful and popular tool of the liturgy. Whether consciously or unconsciously, the post-conciliar interpreters of the hyperactive Holy Spirit followed this counsel. The result was that the most immediate and effective consequence of the kidnapping of the Second Vatican Council was a liturgical revolution. And what emerged from the attendant upheaval was an incomparable victory for the business as usual demands of an uncorrected and untransformed nature.

No one ought to be surprised either by this liturgical revolution or its consequences. We have seen that interwar experiments testified to its imminent arrival. And if personalists insisted that Catholicism was obliged not merely to take into account but to bend unquestioningly to what was defined as the "Spirit of God tending towards convergence" in each and every vital community and culture that it encountered, the Church was equally bound radically to alter her liturgical practices to suit the pressing demands of her vital environment.

But diving into a naturalist atmosphere inevitably had to put men to sleep regarding the full promise of the created world. It had to teach them to end their hunt for nature's "logos" at the uncorrected, passionate, community level — merely the first step in their enlightenment from a Socratic and Word-drenched standpoint. It had to teach them to stop looking for nature's logos at a level that encouraged those communal "happenings" wherein societies worshipped themselves: exactly the kind of liturgical prayer that Rousseau suggested as the expression of the civil religion of the natural, virtuous State. And guidance of worship by what took place at this level alone was a direction ensuring indulgence in all of the evils identified throughout the course of the present work; indulgence both in what Dietrich von Hildebrand called ordinary or "classical" sins, as well as in all the bizarre sicknesses that ideological and libertine madness had discovered and cultivated in man in recent times.

Worse still, liturgy conceived of as a response to uncorrected nature was bound to seek yet more guidance each time a vital, active interpreter of spirits identified yet another energetic community with a message to which an open, pastoral Church must give witness. A Catholicism that continually pursued such novelty, while abandoning, as insensitive prejudice, all education and tradition standing in the way of a wholehearted acceptance of each new message coming in from the external world, was stripped of any means of judging whether it really ought to be ready to incorporate the teachings it received from its environment into the liturgy or not. Indeed, in the long run, its self-dismantling deprived it of any means of nurturing any memory of any doctrinal, philosophical, or historical point of reference to which to relate the liturgy at all.

Even giving the benefit of the doubt to the liturgical proponents of "listening to energetic nature" — presuming, that is to say, that they expected to hear messages basically in line with what they customarily took for granted as True, Good, and Beautiful — the awakened Catholic of an intransigent mentality knew exactly what lay in store from their approach. Turning inward, away from the focus on the truly other, involved, as Dietrich von Hildebrand so well described in *Transformation in Christ*, an ever-deeper plunge into the untutored self; into its temptation to view what was cheapest, most immediately impressionable to the senses, and most parochial as somehow more "real", more rewarding and more expressive of the will of God.

This began, for many contemporary liturgical revolutionaries, by tapping into soldiers' memories of hearing Mass on the back of a jeep, amidst their comrades, with the sounds of artillery around them. Liturgists stirring up such memories contrasted the "truth" of that soldierly experience with the "artificiality" of their liturgical and parish life under normal peacetime circumstances, calling for reform to recapture the lost ties with this more serious "reality". Such a mentality also explained why certain priests in German labor camps, close to the pre-war liturgical movement, treated the hell that they endured therein as providing a more clear and "normal" teaching about the truth of life than the refined peacetime world that had nurtured them.

While in no way denying the potential value of the wretched wartime experience in focusing someone on existential questions, it is necessary to note that its possession of a certain merit is beside the point. The crux of the matter lies in whether or not the experience of overpowering hellishness should become the supreme and sole guide to the construction of the liturgy; whether Christian order should be built upon the vivid context of experienced hell; whether the man who wished to found Christendom upon reflection aiming upwards was merely a slave of a crippled past or the authentic voice of the mission of the Word in history. Modern, personalist-inspired liturgists opted for reality as hell. And this, as Professor David White notes, helps us to explain why our contemporaries devour Dante's *Inferno* while his *Paradiso* goes generally unread. It is because "real nature", for them, is hell, and hell is the defining element of their lives. Were heaven to be opened up before them, they would not want to enter into its precincts. The spirit of the death camp constructed by the doctrine of total depravity guided their whole mind, their whole heart, and their whole soul.

Whatever the case, the post-conciliar liturgical revolution abandoned that primary focus on God that unveiled the full meaning of the Word in history and, by showing nature its true vocation, helped still more to focus human eyes on higher things. The public prayer of the Church was drowned in energetic communal concerns as interpreted by the strongest element most active in shaping devotional life. These concerns diversified *ad infinitum*, as each nation, diocese, parish, and faction within a local community discovered its own startling new spirit, needs, and message to teach. True to the development of the principle of total depravity through modern naturalism, this has meant that the more drab on the one hand and the more grossly sensual on the other, the greater these concerns have been identified with what was thought to be truly "real". A single liturgical revolution thus translated into endless liturgical revolutions "listening" to every "need" from that of the capitalist robber baron to the homosexual—with the former making good money off of the new missals and calendars dictated by each further change in church architecture and ritual practice.

Let us reiterate that such new rites do not emerge spontaneously out of any true—even if misled—communal desire, but, typically, through the revolutionary mediation of vital teachers of the will of the community, who decide what can and cannot be "heard" as the authentic voice of "The People". I once witnessed an example of this phenomenon when I saw a Hispanic community singing traditional hymns to the Madonna silenced so that it could be forced to stutter other unknown tunes, declared by the liturgical experts who had created them *ex nihilo* to be more consonant with the true Latino spirit. Everywhere, the starting principle of the more serious liturgical movement—the need to go back to the ancient sources and their organic development—has given way to a reliance on no teaching other than that of these interpreters of the community will and a demand for "faith" in the spirit and signs of the times that they reveal. And everywhere, anyone criticizing the changes demanded has been chastised not on the basis of what such criticisms really are—a call back to true faith, to objective use of reason, and to a respect for that traditional spirit that any real culture always takes seriously. Instead, their criticisms have been maligned as something racist, elitist, restrictive, anti-pluralist, and, inevitably, fascist. Deny the wishes of the liturgical revolutionaries and the doors of the concentration camp swing open just around the corner.

E. THE DESTRUCTION OF CHRISTENDOM

This now brings us to the question of the political and social effects of the "pastoral" dogmatists. Their approach obviously required a rejection of any organization with the distinct purpose of promoting the corrective and transforming work of the Word in history. It obliged not just Catholic States and political parties but all Catholic Action groups as well to renounce whatever unique religious character they possessed as a precondition for survival. After all, the existence of such a Catholic aura represented an "outside context" and a "contingency" weighing down upon the immediate contemporary vitality of the population of any particular land. The People of God were meant to witness—not to teach a religious or a rational principle. They were meant to witness to the messages that their prophets wished them to bring to perfection "in the Spirit", and *exactly* as those prophets interpreted them. If they did not do so, the court of modernity had once again to proclaim judgment upon them as the philo-fascists they obviously were.

Still, the voluntary abandonment of the Word-drenched mission had to lead to a Catholic subservience to whatever force was most powerful in any given nation, diocese, or parish. If the personalist, pluralist, post-conciliar prophet was already an enthusiastic spokesman for such a force, then all would go well for him, since it would show that he had chosen his vital energy accurately. If he had not read the signs of the times properly—that is to say, if he had not correctly judged who possessed the strongest will in the environment in which he operated—then he had but two options before him. He could bend his message to fit that of the still more powerful force triumphing around him, or he could seek to raise the People's consciousness to his own view through cultivation of some form of underground opposition to the stronger group or individual will.

Whatever the nature of the winning energy, the future for the Catholic peoples of the world was dim. The door to the influence of the libertines and criminals who most benefit from pluralism was opened wide into their communities. Invitations to accommodate themselves to their willful definition of freedom and use it to secure their own illicit desires while still calling themselves Catholic were too enticing for many to turn down. In the meantime, firm believers found that they were pressed to work more openly, more closely, and more approvingly with the dominant elements in the society around them than they had ever been expected to do by any past pontiff or monarch who had overstepped his proper authority. But the nature of this union of conquered Church and Triumphant Will differed somewhat depending upon whether it took place in the United States, in Europe, or in the Third World.

Let us broadly examine the *general* practical results in greater detail with reference first of all to the situation of Catholics in the United States, where pluralism had already long been the civil religion, protected by a host of powerful inquisitors in the courts, the Press, and the educational system. A study of America is especially important given that the model of the United States was supposed to dispel all doubts about the merits of the pluralist methodology as Defender of the Peace and Freedom of the believing Catholic population.[27]

"Diving into" and gaining the graces of the freedom and order offered by the Divine Republic meant obtaining something that "sounded Christian", both because it could easily be related,

---

[27] On Catholicism and the United States, see Mayeur, XII, 833–932; XIII, 255–341; Jedin and Dolan, X, 642–671.

historically, to its fundamental Puritan Protestant roots and because supporters of the Moderate Enlightenment always preferred to keep the language of God in their public speech even after they had lost all traditional faith in Him. We have seen that the system's "godliness" was convincing to American Catholics of the turn of the twentieth century. It seemed even more credible to their post-Second World War descendants, thrilled, as they were, that their country stood out as the chief "God-fearing" nation sheltering the world against atheist Soviet Marxism, and, therefore, the only "practical" alternative to godless Communism. But Catholic Church "freedom" within this system really meant a number of things that had precious little to do with the definition of the term "God-fearing" according to a Tradition that praised the Word over words and equated liberty with correction and transformation in Christ.

First of all, it meant the freedom to rip the communal authority of the Mystical Body of Christ to shreds, reducing it to the status of a religious "club". All attempts to hold onto Church authority and, worse still, to try to use that authority to lead men to Christ, were chastised as assaults on "real freedom", "common sense", and "public order". They were condemnable in the eyes of the anti-institutional, atomistic God of Protestantism, the anti-institutional Nature of the liberty-loving Moderate Enlightenment, and the postwar anti-institutional inquisition permanently on campaign against the revival of fascism.

Commitment to true freedom had therefore to be displayed in a very precise and by now quite familiar two-fold fashion: by a show of contempt for the Church's real self, and through an enthusiastic acceptance of the one unquestionable doctrine guiding human life—an "inclusive" openness to diversity. This was expressed by vigorously favoring whatever had *not* been approved of or encouraged by authentic Catholic tradition. As suggested above, each "open", "inclusive" advance required a new statement of principles, a new program of renewal, a different kind of educational curriculum, and, very frequently, a fresh diversion of ever more limited parish funds to alterations in the physical structure of the local church. These changes always replaced something distinctly familiar with ideas and symbols that were not. And such changes were destined to continue so long as there was something new to "integrate"; even, as Jean Mienveille said, the vital, lived message of the Antichrist himself.[28]

An embrace of the freedom to be inclusive predictably led to the domination of the Catholic branch of the American Pluralist Church by precisely those sort of strong, clever, unscrupulous individuals and groups to which the American scene had historically been inclined to give birth. There is no need to explain once again why and how this resulted in the overwhelming influence of commercial, sexual, and psychologically disturbed crochets, as well as the pseudo societies that promoted and sustained them. I have already indicated that Plato, in *The Republic*, explained this phenomenon much better than I could do here, even without having experienced the history producing such results.

Suffice it to say that openness, freedom, inclusivity and fear of intolerant divisiveness disturbing the peace of the American desert led to the "deconstruction" of even the most sublime Catholic themes on purely sexual grounds; to a concern for justifying everything religious on the basis of its market appeal or adherence to "professional business standards"; to democratic votes determining which doctrines were acceptable in the eyes of charismatic prelates, pastors, religious, theologians, journalists, and certifiable madmen; to the churning of all Catholic life through endless committees, councils, chanceries, and advertising firms, making approach to what were supposed to be compassionate, pastoral-minded, post-conciliar bishops something akin to seeking audience with semi-divine oriental potentates.

---

[28] J. Meinveille, *De Lamennais à Maritain* (La Cité catholique, 1956), on the problems of the "double magisterium", pp. 159–169, 292–293.

Hence, the Catholic branch of the American Pluralist Church came to mirror the war of all against all found everywhere in the atomistic society that it adulated. It regularly intensified this war under the pressure exerted by groups and individuals who expanded the borders of what "common sense" must accept for the sake of peace and consensus. Let us once again remember that it was this "multiplication of factions" constantly battling one another that James Madison praised in the *Federalist* as the special political and social tool of the American Defender of the Peace. Peace, this system certainly has provided, at least for the moment, although the tranquility coming with it has little to do with the "peace that passeth all understanding" that was dear to the Church's former self.

Secondly, individual believers discovered that their apparently radical *personal* as opposed to communal freedom did not guarantee them the right to be "more Catholic than the Church". Given the influence of other powerful elements in American life, that personal freedom also had to be exercised in a way that did not disturb the peace and order preferred by the supporters of the Moderate Enlightenment and their heirs. It also had to be "inclusive" and avoid "divisiveness". Of course individual Catholics had the liberty to present their own varying magisterial teachings for the guidance of their restricted, impotent, cocktail party worlds. Nevertheless, their practical, public, political, social, and economic lives had to be different; more in line with the dismal vision presented to the children victimized in Charles Dickens' *Hard Times*, as expressed by whoever could most powerfully interpret it in their immediate parochial circumstances. Pluralist insistence on separation of thought and action thus gave individual believers the freedom to cultivate a profound psychological disorder; the freedom to become mentally ill; the freedom to live a schizophrenic existence. It is now worth exploring *this* horrible truth at some length.

Fallen man in general already suffers from the temptation to separate purpose and action and then to go along his path to eternity as though such clinical separation were not destructive. Pluralism constructs its whole methodology upon encouragement of this temptation, with major consequences for the unity of the human personality. It praises the man who thinks one thing about his purpose in life and behaves as though his actions in the society around him need not be coordinated with that goal. Hence, it permits him to believe that he has done his duty to the truth and to his conscience if he asserts his convictions about the meaning of existence but avoids the divisive actions in daily life that would give them concrete significance. Most men would like to be courageous but would also appreciate calm and lack of friction with their neighbors. Pluralism provides them a way to have both. It makes courage easy by defining it in a manner that disturbs nothing and no one — least of all the brave men in question and their ordinary routine. Whether a person sees the contradictory situation this prohibition leaves him in or not, it marks him in a way that deforms his personality. It obliges him to turn in upon himself, to deny the crucial importance of his social environment in shaping his destiny, to construct a dike against all energetic action founded upon Faith and Reason, and to declare an introspective sterility to be the normal condition of life. I am, therefore, in no way exaggerating when I say that pluralism literally creates psychological disorders that drive individuals and societies under its influence insane.

Life in a pluralist world has the same disordering effects on even the most well-intentioned Catholics, so much so that they unconsciously prevent Christ from being King over themselves as individuals. Many orthodox bishops, priests, religious, and lay leaders do, indeed, still look for guidance from the Catholic Magisterium. Nevertheless, because they have been formed within a pluralist environment, they are subject to what St. Cyril of Alexandria called *dypsychia*. They have two guiding spirits; two guiding lights. Their Catholic Magisterium is combined with, and ultimately subordinated to, a second, Pluralist Magisterium. It is this

Pluralist Magisterium that shapes their concrete daily actions, their whole way of life, their "second nature." This second Magisterium permits the first to survive, but only in the fashion indicated above: in the private sphere. Thus, as we have seen, it tells them that they have done all that they can legitimately do for their beliefs if they merely talk.

Talk is good, but it is not enough to assure Christ's reign. Popes, prelates, priests, and every living Catholic man, woman, and child could reaffirm and recite every word of every fine catechism, pastoral decree, conciliar and papal pronouncement, and canonical judgment from the time of the apostles down to the present, from dawn until dusk, without it necessarily making a bit of difference in their lives. A simultaneous commitment to the concrete Pluralist Magisterium would show the world that all such talk was simply impotent chatter. If someone lives under the influence of this second Magisterium, he will *act* only with reference to things that it considers important, undercutting the value of what he *says*. A well-intentioned, orthodox Catholic who has digested the messages of pluralist culture that bombard him day in and day out will conclude that he cannot put true Catholic models into practice. He will presume that he must act in a way that pluralism considers to be practical and pragmatic. Pluralism reminds him that theology, philosophy, history and everything else that can really help him to understand the full implications of his Faith for his personal life are not "useful" in our sexualized, commercialized, democratic Empire of the World. This concrete Pluralist Magisterium drives home the argument that all of his fine Catholic words must remain just words lest they become dangerous and divisive. But it also assures him at one and the same time that Catholicism cannot help but prosper in a pluralist society. Hence, it teaches him the "good story" that distorting Christianity along pluralist lines in daily life is the best way to gain benefits for the Faith. In other words, his second Magisterium gives him a dagger to commit religious and cultural suicide. He uses it without ever realizing what he is doing since he is, after all, still reciting the correct orthodox words, in which he firmly believes.

Allow me to offer but a single example. I know of one good bishop — and there are many more like him — who delivers excellent public talks on Catholic catechesis. The Catholic Magisterium is honored in every one of his words. Still, he prides himself on being a practical, pastoral, post-conciliar leader. Therefore, his diocese is filled with practical programs of the kind suggested by the Pluralist Magisterium. But exactly the same type of irrational enthusiasts and willful bureaucrats who dominate unorthodox dioceses administer these programs. Both programs and administrators are focused upon the latest sexual obsessions, the most up-to-date commercial gimmicks, or the best in anti-authoritarian democratic changes. The bishop does not think of stopping their antics, since he, too, has been shaped by pluralism. He fears that actions against them would render him naïve, impractical, undemocratic and divisive. To prove that he has no sympathy for such evil tendencies, he goes out of his way to encourage their projects. The faithful learn from such programs and such stewards exactly what it is that the bishop's orthodox statements really mean in daily life: absolutely nothing. If the faithful try to build their Catholicism upon the innumerable recommendations of diocesan bureaus and spokesmen, they will never have time to investigate Catholic Tradition as a whole, to see whether or not these "practical" projects are actually as good as they are told.

If the dilemma is pointed out to the bishop, he often reacts vigorously, but in a way that aids the pluralist cause and hurts Catholic Tradition still further. He calls attention to his personal orthodoxy, which no one doubts, but which is simply not sufficient to deal with the problems of the diocese. He acts as though his charism as bishop guarantees the legitimacy of pastoral methods that cannot really lay claim to infallibility. If one insists upon the distinction of doctrine and prudential action and continues the critique, making reference to a variety of arguments from Catholic theology, philosophy, history, psychology and sociology to demonstrate what is happening around him, a fideist pluralist bell goes off in his head. He dismisses his critics on pluralist grounds, for closed-minded, divisive attitudes; for lack of "faith" in the methods dictated by the Council and its "spirit." He points to the pope, who points to the Council. Their statements reiterating Catholic doctrine are called forth to assure the critics to have no fear. One might then try to indicate, yet again, that it is not the words of the Council, the pope, and the bishop himself that are under question, at least when these merely repeat orthodox teaching, but the practical, contradictory methodology accompanying them.

Still, once this point has been reached, further discussion is hopeless. Nothing is permitted to bring into question the degree to which such methodology is *de fide* and valid. No rational evidence of what has transpired, in practice, by following it is allowed in court. The bishop insists upon defending the truth and simultaneously encouraging its enemies to subvert it. The new age of freedom and reason within the Church requires Catholics to abandon the free use of their faith and their reason to complain of the destruction of the diocese. At best, the bishop laments the manner in which some people reject "true" pluralism and deny the Catholic Church's right to have her full message heard. But when he does so it is he who is deceived. Many of the very servants he defends are active in smothering that full message and working, consciously or unconsciously, to make sure that Catholics do the only thing that "true" pluralism really permits them to do: emasculate and destroy themselves.

Finally, both the Mystical Body of Christ as an institution and her individual members are given the freedom to thank profusely the powerful, competing, civil religion preached by the American Pluralist Church not only for protecting them better than any other force in human history but for expressing their Catholic beliefs in a more godly fashion as well. This, in one sense, is nothing new. We have repeatedly seen that the Zeitgeist of each and every era produces powerful "traditions" and "customs" of its own, sufficient to influence Catholics eager to "succeed" in their particular environment to ignore and even revile what their real traditions and customs teach them. Supporters of supposedly practical, prudent, pragmatic, successful, and therefore apostolic "traditions", such as the "traditions" of the Sacred Empire, the corrupt papal and episcopal courts and curias of the late Middle Ages, or the Most Christian Kings and Divine Republics of the early modern era, all divinized ideas and practices that were actually not part of Catholic Tradition at all, but, rather, errors and abuses. They all then treated critics of such false traditions as wild-eyed and destructive zealots, even heretics, reminding us, once again, that nothing does more to aid and abet a nightmare than an unwillingness to admit that it really is disturbing our true peace and quiet.

From the end of the nineteenth century, American Catholics were pressured to join this unhappy historical club with greater insistence than ever before. They were more and more raised on the same national heroes, myths, symbols, rituals and sacred texts as their non-Catholic neighbors, and actually fought for these in two world wars. Patriotism seemed to demand that they jell the civil religion of their homeland together with their baptismal faith. Thinkers began to tell them to accept the dicta of the great men of America as Catholic in spirit, if not, indeed, integral to the Deposit of Faith itself; that the Founding Fathers were Doctors of the Church; that "tolerance", as the Founders' hero, John Locke, proclaimed, was the essence of "true" Christianity; that a full embrace of the American "heritage" actually enhanced the "Catholic Moment" in history.

With the added push given by Second Vatican Council and its exposure of Catholics to whatever was the strongest force in the world around them, they now embraced this heritage with wild abandon. A corrupt eighteenth century vision was treated as though it were the perennial message of the Church. Everything desired by Puritan, Whig, and Moderate Enlightenment thought, as transmitted through the will of the Founders of the Divine Republic, gained ecclesiastical blessing. 1776 became the date when grace really entered the world for Catholics as well, leaving all those saints who were transformed in Christ without experiencing its impact lacking in serious foundation for their holiness. For sanctity was achieved not through dancing the dance of life according to the music of the spheres, but by mastering the rhythms suggested by the ever downward spiraling, materialist-inspired "common sense" of the American way of life.

Catholic subservience to the principles of pluralism had another side effect as well. Left to its own devices, the American Religion was bound to wreak havoc with the world that Catholics previously loved. When Catholics attributed the good that they saw in America to the truth of the false ideas guiding their nation, and even declared such ideals to be Catholic ones, they helped to bring on the impending disaster even more swiftly. They ceased to apply that healthy, distinctively Catholic pressure that had contributed to the defense of the remnants of a traditional-minded Protestantism so that both, together, might divert the sickly American tradition away from the logic of its own beliefs and towards more suitable goals. In doing so, they allowed the opportunity for American culture to degenerate more quickly and systematically into the nightmarish nowhere land we see around us today. With nothing uniquely Catholic to contain it, a Protestant-Enlightenment society that had been falsely identified as Catholic-friendly has resulted in what it was bound to produce: a new Sack of Rome.

Let us remember that an all too similar version of this conquest of Catholicism portrayed as the will of the Holy Spirit has played out in Europe as well as in North America.[29] The strong, clever,

[29] Mayeur, XIII, 255–341, 385–425; Jedin and Dolan, X, 505–641.

unscrupulous individuals and groups that have taken advantage of the dismantling of the corrective and transforming mission of the Word in history have varied, due to circumstances, just as much in the Old World as in the New. Still, two variants on the same basic theme should be noted in discussing the situation in Europe.

One involves the fact that, unlike the United States, whose tradition was Protestant from the very outset, Europe had actually once been Catholic. It had also been home to a Greco-Roman culture whose Seeds of the Word had been cherished by a powerful Catholic Church that had, at times, actually tried to accomplish the work that Christ had given her to do. Even if that labor had to a large degree been abandoned over the past few centuries, the imprint of this combined secular and sacred heritage was still there, in many both open and hidden forms. If the notion of a Catholic State seeking the common good, and the concept of a proper role for Catholic parties and Catholic Action had had a lengthy history anywhere, it was in Europe. This meant that the demand for an assault upon that powerful, natural and supernatural teaching had to be, if anything, perhaps still more insistent, brutal, and complete than in an America where rejecting it came more easily. Europeans had to be shown that they were under a special obligation to make one crucial exception to the otherwise inexorable command to accept and bend to the dictates of vital energy. That exception was the vital energy still displayed by Catholic-Greco-Roman culture itself. This alone had absolutely no message to tell anyone. And it had no message for the Old Continent in particular.

Luckily for the supporters of nature as is, the Second World War had already devastated Catholic political parties and much of Catholic Action. Efforts to rebuild the latter in countries where it had once been very powerful, as in Germany, were negligible even before the Council began. Interpreters of the Holy Spirit made sure that whatever Catholic political and social structures were still in place after Vatican Two rapidly disappeared in the name of "human values", pluralism, and the fight against fascism. Concordats based upon the idea of the Church as the Mystical Body of Christ rather than an amorphous People of God manipulated by willful strong men were abandoned. Christian Democratic Parties proved their commitment to openness by serving as the conduits for introducing divorce and abortion into Catholic lands and seeking "historic compromises" with anti-religious forces. Catholic Action groups, where they still existed, were all transformed into versions of the *Grand Sillon*, with emphasis placed upon the technocratic skills required for the work in the media, educational, industrial, and agricultural spheres that they tackled rather than the Catholic Faith and teleological end of the people that might militate in their ranks. Efficient, professional, pragmatic success according to the standards of the naturalist world became the model for a Europe wandering faithlessly through the desert but filled with *gaudium et spes*.

Secondly, when the Council met and for several decades thereafter, there was still a Soviet Bloc to confront. That Bloc was officially guided by a Marxist-Leninist vision that continued to exercise a certain charm over many personalist spokesmen for the Holy Spirit. Moreover, let us remember that thinkers like Jacques Maritain had argued that any problems presented by Marxism-Leninism for the Christian Faith might be transcended if only they were approached with the aid of the pluralist message emerging from the United States. Hence, the post-conciliar passion for an accommodation with the existing system reflected in the so-called *Ostpolitik* pursued by the Vatican during the reign of Pope Paul VI. This policy gave *gaudium et spes* to Pax priests in their efforts to cooperate with the Peoples Republics.

Unfortunately, all this openness was to a "vital energy" that was dying a slow and painfully embarrassing death. Rather than coming to grips with a truly natural reality, what *Ostpolitik* did was to aid in giving credibility to the Marxism of the cynical apparatchiks and political opportunists who more and more dominated the Soviet

Bloc. Hence, rather than helping the cause of devout Soviet Bloc Catholics who continued to suffer from the cynical but still powerful evils of a dying Marxism, *Ostpolitik* merely aided in delaying its inevitable demise. That came, ultimately, from determined confrontation with communist regimes rather than attempts to accommodate them. And when it did come, unemployed apparatchiks and opportunists easily found their way, after the Soviet collapse, into the two fields of activity provided by the pluralist system for the unnaturally ambitious: multi-national corporations and organized crime.

Apart from these two differences, the contemporary conquered European Catholic world looks largely similar to its victimized American Catholic counterpart. This, of course, is not particularly surprising. Given the many common Protestant or Enlightenment influences that Europe shared with the United States, the themes emphasized by the conquered Catholicism of the Old Continent were bound to be largely those same commercial, sexual, and psychologically disturbed cultural crochets, translated into endlessly evolving liturgical and moral revolutions, familiar to Americans. Insofar as European influences were different, pressure from the United States, the homeland of the new Empire of the World, unceasingly helped to direct the consequences of the abandonment of the corrective and transforming message of the Word in history down the path dictated by the culture of the now global Defender of the Peace. Sad to say, the mindlessness that this demanded would eventually wipe out memory of the European past to such a degree that all of the ideological errors bringing on the disasters that made the peace of pluralism attractive to the Old World in the first place could be forgotten and some day perhaps even repeated anew.

We have seen that intransigents were convinced that the naturalist civilization they were fighting inside Europe was guilty of terrible injustice in its dealings with the rest of the globe. Instead of allowing a different world providing further Seeds of the Logos to be corrected and transformed in Christ, Western colonial empires often suppressed legitimate aspects of native cultures or prevented their evangelization for purely utilitarian and power political motives. Intransigent Catholics would therefore not have been surprised by post-colonial movements of all kinds: neither those that reasserted legitimate native pride, nor others that expressed an illegitimate spirit of vengeance, nor still others that proclaimed commitment to one or another ideological development of a false Western naturalism that had made unhappy inroads among them.[30]

Tragically, another outgrowth of Western naturalism, in the form of that twentieth century personalist and pluralist alliance that kidnapped the Second Vatican Council to serve its own agenda, continued to try to manipulate what has become known as the Third World. These Western-bred forces have labored mightily to the detriment of Catholicism in Third World lands. But they have also done so to the detriment of the native cultures that the work of the Word in history truly does respect and can actually bring to as great a fulfillment as it did Europe's classical Greco-Roman heritage. Personalism and pluralism have accomplished this negative activity through the post-conciliar advances of Liberation and Third World Theology. Both of these theologies sought to bend the corrective and transforming message of Christ to the demands of "nature as is": always, of course, as such demands were interpreted by the strongest active wills in a given land, with the prophetic voices of the personalist European heralds of the Holy Spirit chief among them.

Liberation Theology is most associated with Latin America, a vast and very diverse region, composed of countries some of which are almost entirely European, others Indian or Black, and still others highly mixed in population. A number of Latin American nations had developed serious Ninth Crusader movements,

---

[30] Mayeur, XIII, 343–379, 509–741; Jedin and Dolan, X, 352–377; 672–804; P. Letamendia, *Eduardo Frei* (Beauchesne, 1989), pp. 87–232.

including political parties and Catholic Action associations, all of them highly conscious of the importance of corporate and State institutions for individuals living in a properly ordered society seeking the common good. Many activists, such as Garcia Moreno (1821–1875) in Ecuador, were deeply marked by the militant spirit of the intransigents and maintained close ties with the evolution of ideas and initiatives in Europe. This spelled familiarity with and enthusiasm for critiques of the evils of Protestantism and liberal capitalism, both of which were protected in Latin America through the political and cultural influence of Great Britain and the United States. Alas, it also meant familiarity and enthusiasm for the various manifestations of personalism as well.

In Latin America, as elsewhere, the Second Vatican Council encouraged the increased autonomy of regional and national episcopal organizations, along with that of local ordinaries. And just as everywhere else, these proved to be highly susceptible to the self-confident guidance of the voices of the Holy Spirit interpreting the Council according to the wishes of its prophetic, personalist and pluralist conquerors. The voices of Jacques Maritain, with his so-called Integral Humanism, alongside those of the heirs of the Mounier-Uriage school of Vichy France, were especially influential and very active in various Latin American nations' episcopal circles, in the Chilean Christian Democratic Party, and in institutions like the *Instituto Catequistico Latinoamericano*, founded in 1961.

With rapid industrial and agricultural change and the attendant social problems intensifying traditional Catholic irritation with liberal capitalism; with military governments backed by the United States threatening to dominate everywhere; with Christian Democratic Parties expanded to embrace "human values" rapidly failing, the "vital energy" expressed by movements such as those of Fidel Castro and Che Guevara gained more and more support from personalist inspired activists in the region. Personalist thinkers, both European and native, then translated their practical acceptance of the "signs of the times" into that Liberation Theology that the hyperactive Holy Spirit now commanded the Church to embrace and teach.

Liberation Theology, which interpreted the Church's Social Doctrine and the spirit of the Council according to its own time-bound political concerns, proved to be yet another support for "nature as is" in modern, revolutionary form. According to its theorists, the primary need of all men was, not surprisingly, "freedom". Dependency of any kind was the only evil in life. Native freedom in Latin America, they argued, with some justice, had been devastated by much that had happened since Columbus' arrival in 1492. Evils connected with the Industrial Revolution intensified the damage still further. Rather than the Truth that sets men free, however, what was first said to be required to put things straight was a revolution that would liberate the region from the atomistic capitalist system nurtured by the United States and its military henchmen. And insofar as the native population itself did not recognize this to be true, its insouciance was predictably ascribed to its need for a systematic course in "consciousness raising". This could be given it by releasing it from traditional parish bonds and re-organizing it in "base communities" where it could be taught what it *really* felt, in its heart of hearts, by the liberation theologians trained to read its soul. Should it balk at such training, the machine guns of the guerrilla soldiers fighting the fascist proponents of dependency could awaken it to a more suitable response.

Perhaps more significant still for the future of Catholicism in the post-colonial environment was the development of Third World Theology. This emerged out of both Protestant as well as Catholic missionary circles and began, as we have already seen, with concerns regarding "inculturation". Whatever the true merits of inculturation may be — and I think that there are a good number, always connected closely together with the doctrine of the Seeds of the Logos — its historical alliance and its radicalization in the Catholic world in conjunction with personalism and pluralism have been a disaster. Through their influence, any attempt to convert others has been castigated as the product of "racism" and "Eurocentrism" and as an insult to the "felt reality" of the people being evangelized. The very word "missionary" has thereby become a term of abuse.

What the former "missionary" was urged to do was to "give witness" to his Faith unaffected by "outside information", including the entirety of the Christian Tradition and the Socratic tools harmonized with it. By insisting upon an unprejudiced dive into the vital, active milieu in which the "witness" works, no contact with a vital, active historical Christ outside of and above this milieu was permitted. The objective reality of the Incarnate God-Man was thus ultimately called into question, the very concept actually being identified as merely a "Western" understanding of the work of the Spirit in human life. But all cultures are thereby reduced to ultimate meaninglessness, with none being allowed the possibility of making an objective contribution to human life capable of influencing another. All cultures become like ships passing one another in the night, with no philosophy, no theology, and no Christ as polar star above them by means of which they might navigate with precious natural cargo safely from port to port.

"Contextualization" is the term favored by the word merchants in dealing with what remains of the "witnessing" mission. Contextualists are obliged to favor whatever they find alive in native cultures in the lands unfortunate enough to endure their ministrations. Their task is to bring such living realities to their natural perfection. This is true whether one is speaking of religions of blood sacrifice, cannibalism, or the primal significance of the maternal womb. Once again, the call for unquestioning faith in the spirit of God operating in the vital active communities one encounters — unguided by an historical Christ and the objective, corrected achievements of these traditional native cultures themselves — is a recipe for self-lobotomy. It denies all merit to reason and logical judgment, sarcastically denounced by many personalists as more of that useless baggage of the crippled individual who needs to be enticed into the supra-rational vitality of community-minded personhood for his own spiritual benefit. And it is no wonder that they do so! For the more one encourages abandonment to a spirit that neither dogmatic Christian faith nor objective norms of reason and science are allowed to judge, the less one will see what that "spirit of Christ" to which he is obliged to "witness" really is.

Indeed, this could, at times in history, involve something that *is* good and blessed by the hands of God. But practically speaking, in our own time, and under personalist and pluralist influences, it is most often a "spirit" inspired by a libido for the base and the ugly rejected as something sinful or blasphemous by the whole of the Christian Tradition; a "spirit" interpreted by strong willed individuals and groups who themselves arbitrarily determine the essence and contours of the irresistible progress of the Holy Spirit through time. Unfortunately, those who have lost the most in this victorious advance of Third World Theology are the believing and practicing Catholics in such regions. They, like the Greek and Roman Catholics of the ancient world, know the value of the new life that they have found in Christ, even when this required abandonment of previously venerated beliefs and customs. But, then again, their views do not count. Their consciousness needs to be raised. And the Empire of the World is on the side of the bullies in the war between sophist words and the Incarnate Word.

CHAPTER 6

A Time Game End Game

LET US END THIS LENGTHY MEDITATION on a quest for purification gone mad with a "time game". I play such games regularly in dealing with past ages, transposing my sixty-seven years at the moment of writing this text---1951 to 2018---to an earlier era in order better to grasp what kind of influences would have shaped our ancestors living within a similar time frame. A time game of this sort will illustrate the importance of the years 1918–1939 in a way that should resonate quite effectively among traditionalists.

Given the fact that the Roman Forum discussed the topic addressed in this meditation at its Summer Symposium of 2018, let us play the game here, once again utilizing my sixty seven year life span as a model, but conjuring up the image of a man from Brescia, the diocese in Italy in which our program is held. If we place his birth not in 1951 but in 1897, he would have been raised in pre-war Europe, reached conscription age at the time that Italy entered the First World War in 1915, and become a mature adult of twenty-one at its conclusion. The interwar period would thus have been his truly formative professional era.

Our "time game" demands one further speculation. Let us presume that our young man from Brescia is an intelligent Catholic who would have known what the authorities of the Roman Church deemed to be the intellectual and spiritual causes of the First World War and what they were convinced would be needed to achieve a just and lasting peace once it ended. Shaken, like all westerners, by the profundity of the war crisis and its aftermath, we may also conjecture that this young man meditated on the "official" Roman vision in this, his formative era, perhaps questioning its accuracy. Shaped by his own particular circumstances, he may well have mulled over alterations he would make to it if ever given the opportunity to do so. Such a man would have reached my sixty-seven years not in 2018, but in 1964.

Alas, our hypothetical man from Brescia was an actual historical reality. He was Giovanni Batista Montini (1897–1978), born into a family with its own rather critical outlook on contemporary Catholic life, educated for the priesthood under circumstances different from that of most seminarians, and destined for a formative ecclesiastical career at the center of power of the Roman Church in the interwar period. Montini was eager for Italian entry into the First World War, lest it miss participation in this "vital" activity. He visited monasteries engaged in liturgical experimentation soon after the conflict's end. As the sometime Ecclesiastical Assistant for the Specialized Catholic Action movement of FUCI, one of whose student members, Aldo Moro (1916–1978), became a life-long friend, he became known for his disapproval of a number of official intellectual approaches and pious devotional practices. An appreciation for "something different" was stimulated still further by an enthusiasm for Jacques Maritain's Integral Humanism and aspects of the New Theology.

In 1964, as the sixty-seven year old Paul VI (1963–1978), Montini was in the midst of putting the visions that he nurtured in the interwar period into practice. Moreover, he was doing so with the aid of a battery of fellow prelates and theologians, many sharing almost exactly the same time frame as his own, and, thus, the identical historical background that had stimulated his personal desire for change. Their understanding of what would bring about a true purification of the Church and the world was not that of the nineteenth century Catholic revival movement.

Paul VI died in August of 1978, at least partially under the shock of seeing the real effects of this approach: that of allowing a superhuman "Mynheer Peeperkorn"—Satan—to move into a position of strength in the Church as a whole. The pope's decline and death were most certainly also stimulated by having lived to see his interwar protégé, Aldo Moro, the Christian Democratic leader famous for seeking an "Historic Compromise" with the Italian Communist Party, murdered by Red Brigades, themselves outraged by such pointless dialogue, just three months earlier.

Desperately trying to avoid admitting the real cause of the disasters in both Church and State, the depressed pontiff honored his deceased comrade by repetition of the empty mantras of the new age. "We have kept the faith!" he insisted. "We have kept the faith, I can say today, with the humble but firm consciousness of never having betrayed the Holy Trinity". Paul VI may well have wished these empty mantras to be true, but they simply did not represent the reality. What he and his colleagues had done was to leave the Church, as Maritain feared that the most dangerous forms of personalism would inevitably do, "barren in the face of a Ramkhrishna"; exposed to manipulation by all of the irrational, willful forces discussed above. More than this, the errors of personalism and pluralism have lulled Catholics into the deep, anti-intellectual, naturalist sleep mentioned in the first paragraph of this essay, with its antipathy to history, its lessons, and, their guide back to dogmatic and pastoral sanity.

Fourteen years intervened between Paul VI's sixty-seventh birthday and his death in 1978, long enough for him to see—in his mind, if not necessarily in his heart and his words—the end result of his labors. Let us hope that we, fourteen years from my comparable age today, may live to see the happier conclusion to our battle against the nightmare that Paul VI had begun to cultivate in the interwar period. And if this does not happen, let us pray that we will at least take our final breath having kept the faith with the True Faith.

Ernst Jünger, points the way to how we, in our current powerlessness, can maintain our spirits. He does so in his powerful work of 1939 *On the Marble Cliffs*. His protagonists here are two brothers horrified by the triumph of the barbaric will of a tyrant identified as the *Oberförster* over the civilized order of a place called the Marina. The first step of these heroes is to make an "inner break" with the degenerating ethos of the Marina itself; that inner break that seems so defeatist to the mindless activist but actually is the spiritual mainstay of anyone oppressed by the brute force of overwhelming might. In their "retirement", the brothers return *ad fontes*, to the sources, and dedicate themselves to the study of nature. They know that they will some day have to fight the *Oberförster*, and with an odd conglomerate of seemingly dubious and compromised allies. They are ready to accept this perilous coalition because their peculiar future comrades all still have a clear, underlying sense of the tyrant's evil, and because the heroes know that they themselves were once "part of the problem" that these forces represent. They, like Jünger in his real life involvement with parochial-minded nationalist organizations, had once "ridden with the Mauritanians" — one of the groups that may, unwittingly, have aided the *Oberförster's* rise. But they, like their future frontline friends, had proven to be open to change, and they know, as brother Otho says, that an error only becomes disastrous if men stubbornly persist in refusing to correct it. When they ride off again, it is with this band of brothers in a battle against demonic willfulness. Despite the odds, they ride off in a spirit of *Heiterkeit*; a spirit of cheerful serenity; a Catholic Christian spirit.

Jünger's vision was still flawed when he wrote *Auf den Marmorklippen*, because he had not yet come to that Catholic Faith and the Catholic vision of purification, which he finally did accept in the last years of his very long life. But believers should certainly take heed of the message of the very modern "Seed of the Logos" that his novel offers them. Men like Jünger's heroes and their allies are lost and wandering in our age as perhaps never before. Migrants are to be found everywhere, both physically as well as intellectually and spiritually. Some of these migrants wandering through the desert we call modernity will strive to understand the Logos of things. New Socrates will emerge to guide them on a rational journey toward the light; towards ultimate supernatural correction and transformation in Christ. Believers in the Word Incarnate who nurture the true Catholic pilgrim spirit will recognize them as allies and will welcome them in their midst. They will join in the fight against the *Oberförster*. But their involvement will only be a healthy one so long as we maintain our distance from their errors and our commitment both to an unchanging doctrinal solidity and a humble, self-critical, correction of our pastoral mistakes. Our potential allies are not our Redeemers and can never be treated as such. It is we, as Catholics, who possess the Light of the world.

Let us now end this overly long meditation on a quest for purification gone mad. It has taken us across a vast terrain. Let us complete our journey with a touch of *Heiterkeit*, somewhat playfully and fancifully perhaps, but seriously enough, given the nightmare through which we are still struggling, by mulling over in our own situation the last words of Thomas Mann to Hans Castorp in the trenches in 1914 in *The Magic Mountain*:

> Farewell — and if thou livest or diest! Thy prospects are poor. The desperate dance in which thy fortunes are caught up will last yet many a sinful year; we should not care to set a high stake on thy life by the time it ends. We even confess that it is without great concern that we leave the question open. Adventures of the flesh and in the spirit, while enhancing thy simplicity, granted thee to know in the spirit what in the flesh thou scarcely couldst have done. Moments there were, when out of death, and the rebellion of the flesh, there came to thee, as thou tookest of thyself, a dream of love. Out of

this universal feast of death, out of this extremity of fever, kindling the rain-washed evening sky to a fiery glow, may it be that Love one day shall mount?

BIBLIOGRAPHY

Agócs, Sándor, *The Troubled Origins of the Italian Catholic Labour Movement* (Wayne State, 1988).

Alcobaca, V. de, *What Portugal Owes to Dr. Salazar: A Debt of Gratitude* (Editorial Imperio, 1935).

Allitt, P., *Catholic Intellectuals and Conservative Politics in America, 1950–1985* (Cornell, 1995).

Amerio, R., *Iota Unum* (Sarto, 1997).

Anderson, R., *Between Two Wars. The Study of Pope Pius XI* (Franciscan Publications, 1978).

Arbuthnott, A., *Joseph Cardijn* (London, 1966).

Arnal, O.L., *Ambivalent Alliance: The Catholic Church and the Action Française, 1899–1939* (Books Demand, 1985).

Atkin, N., *Church and State in Vichy France, 1940–1944* (Cambridge, 1991).

Black, G.D., *Catholic Crusade Against the Movies, 1940–1975* (Cambridge, 1998).

Blet, P., *Pius XII and the Second World War* (Paulist, 1999).

Blom, P., *The Vertigo Years: Europe, 1900–1914* (Basic Books, 2008).

Bonneterre, D., *Le mouvment liturgique* (Fideliter, 1980).

Boyer, J., *Culture and Political Crisis in Vienna. Christian Socialism in Power, 1897–1918* (Chicago, 1995).

Bruneau, T.C., *The Political Transformation of the Brazilian Catholic Church* (Cambridge, 1974).

Bulletin (Lisbon: Informacio Nacional).

Carron, J., *Le Sillon et la démocratie chrétienne, 1894–1910* (Plon, 1967).

Chelini, J., *L'église sous Pie XII* (Fayard, Two Volumes, 1983, 1989).

Chiron, Y., *La vie de Maurras* (Goderoy de Bouillon, 1999).

Chiron, Y., *Paul VI. Le pape écartelé* (Perrin, 1993).

Cholvy, G., *Jeunesses chrétiennes au xxe siècle* (Ouvrières, 1991).

La Civiltà Cattolica (Rome, 1918–1939).

Cointet, M., *L'église sous Vichy, 1940–1945* (Perrin, 1998).

Conway, J., *The Nazi Persecution of the Churches* (Regent, 1997).

Conwary, M., *Catholic Politics in Europe: 1918–1945* (Routledge, 1997).
Coolidge, C., "Address to the American Society of Newspaper Editors, Washington, D.C.," January 17, 1925. Online by Gerhard Peters and John T. Woolley, The American Presidency Project. http://www.presidency.ucsb.edu/ws/?pid=24180.
Cotta, F., *Economic Planning in Corporative Portugal* (P.S. King & Son, Ltd., 1937).
Cross, L.D., *The Emergence of Liberal Catholicism in the United States* (Books Demands, 1958).
Davies, M., *The Liturgical Revolution* (Angelus Press, Three Volumes, 1980).
Dawson, A., *The Birth and Impact of the Base Ecclesial Community and Liberative Theological Discourse in Brazil* (International Scholars, 1998).
De Franciscis, M.E., *Italy and the Vatican: The 1984 Concordat Between Church and State* (P. Lang, 1989).
Dominguez, J., *The Roman Catholic Church in Latin America* (Garland, 1994).
Dubarle, D., ed., *Le Modernisme* (Beauchesne, 1980).
Dupuis, J., *Vers une nouvelle théologie chrétienne du pluralisme religieux* (Cerf, 1997).
École Française de Rome, ed., *Achille Ratti. Pape Pie XI* (École Française, 1996).
Fattorini, E., *I cattolici tedeschi dall'intransigenza alla modernità, 1870–1953 (*Morcelliana, 1997).
Ferm, D.W., ed., *Third World Liberation Theologies: A Reader* (Orbis, 1988).
Ferrari, S., *Vaticano e Israele dal secondo conflitto mondiale alla guerra del golfo* (Bologna, 1991).
Ferro, A. *Salazar: Portugal and Her Leader* (Faber & Faber, Ltd., 1939).
Fisher, J.T., *Catholic Counterculture in America, 1933–1962* (Books Demand, 1999).
Gamber, K., *The Reform of the Roman Liturgy* (Una Voce, 1993).
Gariboldi, G.A., *Pio XII, Hitler e Mussolini. Il Vaticano fra le dittature* (Mursia, 1988).
Garnier, C., *Salazar: An Intimate Portrait* (Farrar, Strauss & Young, 1954).
Gilson, E., *The Philosopher and Theology* (Random House, 1962).
Goodrich-Clarke, N., *The Occult Roots of Nazism* (NYU, 1985).

Gregory, J.D., *Dollfuss and His Times* (Hutchinson & Co., Ltd., 1935).
Guasco, M., *Romolo Murri e il modernismo* (Rome, 1968).
Gutiérrez, G., *Théologie de la libération* (Lumen Vitae, 1974).
Hamer, J., *Karl Barth* (Westminster, 1962).
Hellman, J., *Emmanuel Mounier and the New Catholic Left* (McGill-Queens, 1997).
Hellman, J., *The Knight Monks of Vichy France: Uriage, 1940–1945* (McGill-Queens, 1997).
Hildebrand, D. von, *Liturgy and Personality* (Longmans, 1943).
Hunsiger, G., ed., *Karl Barth and Radical Politics* (Philadelphia, 1976).
Invernizzi, Marco, *Il movimento cattolico in Italia* (Mimep-Docete, 1995).
Invernizzi, Marco, *L'Unione elettoralec cattolica italiana* (Cristianità, 1993).
Jedin, H., and Dolan, J., *History of the Church* (Crossroads, Ten Volumes, 1981).
Kay, H., *Salazar and Modern Portugal* (Hawthorn, 1969).
Kenny, A.J., *Catholics, Jews, and the State of Israel* (Greenwood, 1979).
Klemperer, K. von, *Ignaz Seipel. Christian Statesman in a Time of Crisis* (Princeton, 1972).
Knight, A., *The Mexican Revolution* (Cambridge, Two Volumes, 1986).
Launay, M., *Le syndicalisme chrétien en France de 1885 à nos jours* (Desclée, 1984).
Launey, Marcel, *La papauté à l'aube du xx siècle* (Cerf, 1997).
Lemberts, E., *La démocratie chrétienne dans l'Union européene* (Louvain, 1996).
Letamendia, P., *Eduardo Frei* (Beauchesne, 1989).
Lijphart, A., *The Politics of Accommodation. Pluralism and Democracy in the Netherlands* (Berkeley, 1975).
London Times, (2 August, 1934).
Lynch, E., *Religion and Politics in Latin America: Liberation Theology and Christian Democracy* (Praeger, 1991).
McLeod, H., *Religion and the People of Western Europe, 1789–1989* (Oxford, 1998).
Mary, V., *Catholics in the Second Spanish Republic,* (Oxford, 1996).
Mayeur, J.M., ed., *Histoire du Christianisme* (Desclée, Thirteen Volumes, 1990–2002).
Meinvieille, J., *De Lamennais a Maritain* (La Cité Catholique, 1956).
Messner, J., *Dollfuss: An Austrian Patriot* (Burns, Oates & Washbourne, Ltd., 1935).

Moody, J.N., ed., *Church and Society: Catholic Social and Political Thought and Movements, 1789-1950* (New York, 1953).
The New Austria, (Bundeskommisariat für Heimatdienst, 1937).
Nitti, F.S., *Catholic Socialism* (Gordon, 1976).
Partin, M.O., *Waldeck-Rousseau, Combes, and the Church: The Politics of Anti-Clericalism, 1899-1905* (Duke, 1969).
Paul, H.W., *The Second Ralliement* (Washington, 1965).
Peters, W.H., *The Life of Benedict XV* (Bruce Publishing Co., 1959).
Petit, H., L'Eglise, *le Sillon et l'Action Française* (Nouvelles éditions latines, 1998).
Portugal: The New State in Theory and in Practice (SPN, 1938).
Poulat, E., *Intégrisme et catholicisme integral* (Paris, 1969).
Poulat, E., *Catholicisme, démocratie et socialisme. Le mouvement catholique et Mgr. Benigni de la naissance du socialisme à la victoire du fascisme* (Casterman, 1977).
Poulat, E., *Histoire, dogme, et critique dans la crise moderniste* (Albin Michel, 1996).
Poulat, E., *Les prêtres-ouvrièrs* (Cerf, 1999).
Power, M., *Jacques Maritain (1882-1973). Christian Democracy and the Quest for a New Commonwealth* (America, 1997).
Rao, J., "Catholicism, Liberalism, and the Right: a Sketch from the 1920s", http://jcrao.freeshell.org/CatholicismandtheRight.html.
Rao, J., *Black Legends and the Light of the World* (Remnant Press, 2012).
Rhodes, A., *The Vatican in the Age of the Dictators, 1922-1945* (London, 1973).
Riccardi, A., *Il Vaticano e Mosca* (Laterza, 1993).
Romanto, G., *Pio X* (Rusconi, 1992).
Rossi, J.S., *American Catholics and the Formation of the United Nations* (University Press, 1993).
Rumi, G., ed., *Benedetto XV e la pace* (Morcelliana, 1990).
Salazar, A., *Doctrine and Action* (Faber & Faber, 1940).
Salazar, A., *The Principles and Work of the Revolution* (Segretariado da Propaganda Nacional, 1943).
Salazar, A., *The Road for the Future* (SIN, 1962).
Sarasella, D., *Modernismo* (Editrice bibliografica, 1995).
Scaglia, G.B., *La stagione montaniana* (Studium, 1993).
Schultenover, D.G., *A View From Rome. On the Eve of the Modernist Crisis* (Fordham, 1993).

Schuschnigg, K. von, *My Austria* (Alfred A. Knopf, 1938).
Scoppola, P., *La chiesa e il fascismo, Documenti e interpretazioni* (Bari, 1967).
Shepard, G.B., *Dollfuss* (Macmillan & Co., Ltd., 1961).
Sunkler, B., *Nathan Söderblom, His Life and Work* (Uppsala, 1968).
Teixeira, L., *Profile of Salazar* (SPN, 1938).
Thayer, John A., *Italy and the Great War* (University of Wisconsin, 1964).
Tresmontant, C., *La crise moderniste* (Paris, 1979).
Weber, E., *Action Française* (Stanford University, 1962).
Weigel, H. , *Kraus: Die Macht der Ohnmacht* (Brandstätter, 1986),
Wenger, A., *Rome et Moscou, 1900-1950* (Paris, 1987).
Wiltgen, R.M., *The Rhine Flows into the Tiber* (Tan, 1991).
Wolff, R.J., and Hoensch, J.K., *Catholics, the State, and the European Radical Right* (Atlantic Research, 1987).
Zeldin, T., *France, 1848-1945* (Oxford, Four Volumes, 1979-1981).

Also available from
AROUCA PRESS

Meditations for Each Day
Antonio Cardinal Bacci (pbk & hb)

Fraternal Charity
Fr. Benoît Valuy, S.J.

The Epistle of Christ:
Short Sermons for the Sundays of the Year
on Texts from the Epistles
Fr. Michael Andrew Chapman

Our Lady, A Presentation for Beginners
Dom Hubert van Zeller, O.S.B.

Integrity, Volume 1:
The First Year (October–December 1946)
Ed. Carol Jackson, Ed Willock

www.ingramcontent.com/pod-product-compliance
Lightning Source LLC
Chambersburg PA
CBHW060400080526
44583CB00012B/405